ANNA HAUGH'S

Irish Kitchen

*To Liz Dunne, the woman who saw the chef in me
before I even knew I was one.*

ANNA HAUGH'S

Irish Kitchen

MODERN HOME COOKING WITH IRISH HEART

Photography by Laura Edwards

Interlink Books
an imprint of Interlink Publishing Group, Inc.
Northampton, Massachusetts

Introduction

I was lucky to cook alongside my mother as soon as I could stand, and, from the first day I helped her to make dinner in our bright orange kitchen in Tallaght, Dublin, I loved it. Cooking is in my bones and sharing is in my nature. Everything about cooking suited me—and still does – from the wonderful aromas lifting from the pans and the sneaky tastes you can steal as you cook, to the fact that I am always at my best when keeping myself busy.

My mother cooked everything from scratch for the four of us children, while my dad took me to street markets, butchers and fishmongers for the raw ingredients. We had homemade jam, with our own fruits that we grew out in the backyard. We ate local fish from fishmongers who my father would chinwag the day away with. Often, I'd be in the vegetable market with Dad buying pears and oranges by the crateful and potatoes in 25 kg (55 lb) bags, before cheerily sitting in the back of the car as he dropped a few kilos off to his brothers and sisters around town.

I was raised in a house full of music. We children would wake up in the morning to records playing. Mom would do her rounds opening all the bedroom windows (she loved a good airing of the house), and, if the freezing cold didn't wake you up, the music would. Sometimes it was Elkie Brooks, at others Van Morrison or Eric Clapton. On weekend mornings, we would shuffle downstairs in our PJs to the aroma of a Full Irish Breakfast in the works. My mom would say, "Morning, lovey," offer each of us a sausage on a fork and we would plop ourselves down as close to the TV as we were allowed to watch cartoons and eat our sausages, while waiting for Dad to get back from the bakery with the bread. (As with most families, this wasn't a totally idyllic scene: often, we kids would be arguing; sometimes, we would be aiming to land a sly pinch or kick on each other without our parents spotting it...)

My mother thought she was "just" making food for us, but, looking back, I sense the warm embrace of feeling truly loved and nurtured. In a time when we think it's pzazz and wacky bubblegum cupcakes that make a childhood special, it's actually the intention behind what you give that makes family time glorious.

Out of that sunny orange kitchen flew mackerel coated with oats and fried, boxty potato pancakes, Dublin coddle filled with sausages and (yes) potatoes, Irish stew, lamb chops, a seemingly endless supply of fresh scones, and always apple tart cooked on a large dinner plate.

But it wasn't all plain sailing in the kitchen for Mam. She had to navigate a brief rebellious period that followed me staying with friends and eating what their parents cooked for them. I became (briefly) enamored with their packaged sauces and microwave meals; I spurned homegrown jam and wanted store-bought. This was a fleeting misstep, quickly rectified once I tasted the foods I thought I wanted. My mother's recipes are simple, but, as I realized, they are undoubtedly delicious.

These days there is no meal I'd rather be part of than having my parents, my siblings and now our children all sit together and eat. We play music and argue, then move on and laugh and get emotional, because we are all still growing and changing. The same as happens at the kitchen table in so many other households.

But what is served on that table has changed with the years. I remember the first time my mother made spaghetti bolognese for my father, back in the late 1980s. We children had eaten this delicacy a few times before and knew it was delicious, but my father's face dropped as the serving dish came to the table. He asked, "Ah Wendy, where is the meat? Where are the vegetables? And tell me, where are the potatoes?" I am not joking when I say my father was afraid of this dinner: it was alien to him. Anyone who knows my dad will tell you he now adores good pasta; Irish food has come so far from the meat-and-two-veg of just a few decades ago and it is so exciting to be part of this food revolution. For a long time, Irish cooking languished in the doldrums: overlooked both by us Irish—not as mindful of its heritage as we might have been—and by everyone else. Happily, in recent years, the mood couldn't be more different. Irish food has everything to offer: wonderful ingredients with impeccable provenance and rich traditions, as well as a dynamic approach to modernity.

I opened Myrtle, my first restaurant, in Chelsea in London in 2019. The name was inspired by legendary Irish chef Myrtle Allen, founder of famous restaurant and food hub Ballymaloe House in Cork, which has done so much for Irish food. I take humble old Irish recipes and make lighter, more elegant modern dishes that remind people of childhood flavors. I am very proud that, both at my restaurant and in this book, I've been able to adapt my mother's classic recipes to show you what modern Irish cooking really is.

Every cuisine is based on what a country's people ate once upon a time and the ways in which we interpret that today. The humble dumpling appears as gnocchi in Italy, pierogi in Poland and boxty in Ireland. Similarly, moving on to eggs, we have the tortilla in Spain, the frittata in Italy and the Wicklow pancake in Ireland. Irish food is just as worthy of praise, and of study, as that of our more renowned neighbors.

I'm now a restaurant owner and regularly on television as a cooking expert, but believe me when I tell you that the last twenty-odd years of my life in the kitchen have been peppered with mistakes. In fact, that is what I believe real success stands on. All great cooks and chefs have confidence *because* they have split a mayonnaise or overcooked a steak. They know what to avoid when it comes to choosing the right ingredients, because they have tasted an out-of-season strawberry and compared it to a strawberry picked in the warm summer months and eaten shortly afterwards. They know getting the fruit directly from the farm will make it easier for them to create something fantastic. That knowledge can only come through experience, which means trial and error.

My career started almost by accident while on a summer job in Jersey. I was working in a café with a bunch of young ones all around my age and, basically, was having the summer of my life: freedom from my parents and earning money to allow me to do what I wanted. The café was directly connected to the restaurant's kitchen, a door I had never walked through. One day, I was asked to open a few cans of fruit cocktail. So I went into the kitchen... and something just clicked inside—a true eureka moment—and I flew home and burst through the door to tell my parents that I wanted to be a chef. Initially, they weren't overly impressed, and expected that my love of partying would soon make me give up this labor-intensive career choice. But my passion for eating, cooking and teaching people about food won out.

So I enrolled in a professional cooking course at the DIT School of Culinary Arts and Food Technology—commonly known as Cathal Brugha Street—back in Dublin, and my professional chef career began. I started my apprenticeship at the city's L'Ecrivain restaurant under chef Derry Clarke, then soon moved to Paris to work for the famous Italian chef Gualtiero Marchesi at Hotel Lotti. My French wasn't great—and my Italian nonexistant—but it was a very exciting kitchen to be in. I probably learned more while there than in any other kitchen. I also picked up a lot about living within a budget and how to cook at home with very few resources in a kitchen the size of a dining table for two in my restaurant now. I moved to London about nineteen years ago and, while working in the city for Philip Howard, Shane Osborn and Gordon Ramsay, I learned that choosing the right ingredients at the right time can result in not only a delicious dish but a beautiful one, too. While working for those chefs, I began to understand when a plate needs more or, very often, less. They were all busy, emotionally driven restaurants. (One idea I find laughable is that women are too emotional for the job of chef; my decades of experience working almost exclusively with men has taught me that they are very emotional... but that's a book for another day.)

While I was training, I chose to work in kitchens that were busy; I was alive with curiosity and excited to understand my trade. The key word there is *understand*. At no point did I ever dream or aspire to be a head chef, or to appear on television. For many, many years, all I wanted was to be good at my job and there was very little positive reinforcement from my bosses. If I could whisper in young Anna Haugh's ear, I might encourage her to be kinder to herself and a little happier with her own work.

I can't do that for her, but I can whisper in your ear now and encourage you to pick yourself up if you have made a mistake, either while cooking or in any other area of your life. Success does not come quickly and it does not stay unless you continue to invest in it. So, my advice to anyone working hard and not seeing results is to stay calm, keep going and remember that, eventually, you will get out what you put in. I truly believe in fairness, hard work and integrity. Working on all three through thick and thin has given me a grounded sense of pride over the years. It's also taught me a lot about cooking and that's what I want to share now.

Often, home cooks can imagine that cooking is complicated and that professional chefs are the only ones who know how to create magic in recipes, but that's not at all correct: if you enjoy eating and delighting in flavor, you're already halfway there. My goal with this book is to demystify the secrets of great cooking for you.

To that end, from every city I've worked in, I've kept a battered, scrappy notebook crammed with the dishes and kitchen secrets I learned there. In this book, I've combined those classic recipes—as well as others from my own family—with my top insider's tips for how you can create delicious, beautiful plates of food at home with minimal fuss, and how you can elevate them to restaurant standard. Throughout, I've added my best kitchen hacks in the form of my "Tricks of the Trade," which will allow you to understand the processes of cooking and make your recipes taste even better. In these pages, I will explain to you the importance of feeding the eye with different colors, textures and heights on a plate. Follow these flavor-packed, delicious and relatively easy recipes and your dishes can both taste and look like a professional chef created them.

Some of the recipes are best for family sharing, while others are piled high and show-stopping. Others still celebrate the fact that, sometimes, less is more. In bringing together the dishes in this collection, I surprised myself with the variety of recipes that I cook often at home. Some of them are classics with a twist, and there are a few that might be new to you, but what they all have in common is that they are each a labor of love, given from me to you.

Over the years, I've shared recipes with friends and family, and it brings me so much joy when they tell me that they still use them time and again and that they're now on regular rotation in their homes. This book is my way of sharing recipes with you, too. These are dishes that are cooked from my heart, and, when you try them, I want to help you to feel that same heartbeat yourself.

I believe a cookbook is something you can pass down to your kids, filled to bursting with your family-favorite recipes. While I was growing up, back in that orange kitchen, Mam had all of Darina Allen's cookbooks (Darina is the daughter-in-law of Myrtle, and also a famous alumnus of Ballymaloe House). They were small, contrasting-colored books, each devoted to a different subject, such as meat, fish or desserts, and they were in constant use. When I was about 19, my mother bought me my first cookbook: *The Naked Chef*, by Jamie Oliver. To this day, I still approach certain recipes because of what I learned from that book.

So why would I write a cookbook? The dual-part answer is like the two prongs of a carving fork: they only work in unison. I have a burning need to share the secrets of cooking food that has brought so much pleasure, yes, but I also want to tell you about me, my family and the people who have brought me joy and stability. Stories of happiness and solutions. Life has many burdens, but food can help us escape them. Through cooking, we can pass beautiful memories on to our children, friends and the other people we love. Through home cooking, we can nourish our bodies and feel a huge sense of achievement.

You don't need to spend a fortune or be left with a mountain of mess, but even if that does happen, you will have the satisfaction of having done something great for your mind and your body. So just find a helper, stick some music on and tidy up together, to make a positive, sunny memory.

I love cooking food, but not nearly as much as I love giving food to the people who are dear to me. That drive has spilled over into this book. Nothing would bring me more pleasure than knowing you use my cookbook again and again. I hope that the pages get splashed with oil and covered with the scribbled notes that turn my recipes into yours; notes of what works for you (and what doesn't), and what alterations you make when you cook a recipe again. So dig in and enjoy!

Anna Haugh

Tools of the Trade

ESSENTIAL

KNIVES

I'm often asked about knives and here is the answer I give, distilled from a lifetime of kitchen work. You need a knife with a good enough quality blade that it can be resharpened over and again. The Victorinox brand are very durable and, for the price, excellent. It's these that I suggest the novice commis chefs in my restaurant should buy. I still have my Victorinox knives from my commis chef days, the same that I used when I learned how to fillet fish and chop vegetables.

OFFICE KNIFE
This might seem like just an ordinary small knife, but, if kept sharp, it is extremely hard-working and versatile. Useful not just for cutting small items, but also—as a money-saving trick—to prep meat, if you haven't yet invested in a boning knife.

TOMATO KNIFE
A game changer: its serrated "chainsaw" blade is great for cutting bread, all fruit and veg, as well as cooked meats. And tomatoes, of course. However, this isn't the right knife for raw meat or fish, as it will saw rather than cleanly cut flesh.

TONGS

These will help you both to avoid burning your fingers and to work faster. If you invest in silicone tongs, they will protect your nonstick pans, too.

WOODEN SPOON

The humblest of tools, but, centuries after their creation, cooks continue to benefit from them. Hard-wearing yet affordable, I use a wooden spoon to "feel" the cooking through its movement and the sensations transmitted through the handle. In my restaurant kitchen, we use only wooden spoons to make risottos, to sense the texture of the rice. They are also very handy for checking if sauces such as custard are ready, again by feeling and looking for their thickness and consistency while stirring.

SPEED PEELER

You should be able to pick up a speed peeler for a couple of bucks and they are excellent, both at the obvious job of peeling but also for creating strips of vegetables or shavings of cheese to zhuzh up the appearance of your food. They will decrease the time it takes you to prepare dishes, and they make a great starting point for making super-thin slices before investing in a mandoline.

GOOD BOX GRATER

Very useful to help speed up food prep time if you want to avoid chopping everything by hand. It will also save money, as packaged pre-grated cheese costs more than the ungrated block kind.

SIEVE

For sifting flour and cocoa, but also for straining stocks and custard and passing fruit purées through, to remove their seeds.

WHISK

A humble hand whisk costs little to buy; it takes more time to whisk ingredients manually than it does when you use electric versions, but this is a useful tool to have.

PLATES AND DISHES

I'm sure you haven't been eating directly off kitchen surfaces, so I'm assuming you've got these already...

MINI SPIDER STRAINER OR SLOTTED SPOON

So handy when blanching and refreshing vegetables, but also when you are poaching anything that needs to be handled with care.

HANDHELD IMMERSION BLENDER

Hand or stick blenders are now easy to find and inexpensive, and you will need them to make soup or blend mayonnaise.

USEFUL

WOODEN CHOPPING BOARD

Invest in a good board and you will enjoy the prepping process more, as well as protect your knives. It doubles up as a great way to present antipasti or cheese, and, the older it gets, the more personality it develops. It has been proven that wooden boards, when cleaned regularly, can halt bacterial growth far more efficiently than plastic or glass boards.

DIGITAL THERMOMETER

Very useful when checking if food is cooked, but also indispensable when cooking slowly at exact temperatures.

SPATULA

This helps you to protect food that is too delicate to lift out of a pan with a spoon, such as (obviously) a piece of fish, or maybe a hash.

MICROPLANE

Excellent for finishing dishes with a more elegant touch, such as adding a cloud of feather-like Parmesan, or even fine slivers of truffle.

MANDOLINE

Always use the guard! A mandoline will allow you to slice perfectly and to a consistent thickness. There are different settings and teeth to use, so you can easily perform numerous different cutting techniques in a fraction of the time they would take by hand.

MORTAR AND PESTLE

Excellent for grinding spices and making pestos.

NEXT LEVEL

FISH KNIFE

A flexible knife that will help you navigate the bones when filleting and trimming fish.

BONING KNIFE

A rigid knife that you will need if you regularly take meat off the bone.

TWEEZERS

These are good for more intricate plating. They take a bit of practice to master, but in the long run are worth it if you want to present plates with precision.

VACUUM SEALING MACHINE

An investment, for those who are looking to add more technical, consistent and controlled cooking to their kitchens.

WAFFLE MAKER

More useful than you may think. You can use it to make the obvious sweet batter waffles for breakfast or dessert, but also for potato waffles, or even a more greens-rich savory version based on grated zucchini.

HIGH-POWERED BLENDER

These will get your purees silky-smooth, and using one tends to be the difference between restaurant and domestic purées.

20-Minute Dinners

Cooking is a pleasure, but time is not something we all have in abundance. So to start off the book, I wanted to share recipes that don't take long, but which taste like you've been cooking all day. When you need something speedy and yummy, these are the dishes you want.

The more you cook, the faster you become at getting through the prep work of chopping and whisking. But until you get to that stage, I'd suggest saving longer, more elaborate recipes for those days when you can give yourself the time and space to enjoy the process.

I am not a fan of cookbooks that focus on the pains of cooking, the dread of dish-washing, or include recipes that are dumbed down to entice people to cook them. However, like everyone, I have many days where there isn't enough time to spend hours in the kitchen preparing a feast, so in this chapter I'm sharing with you the meals I cook at home when I am in a hurry. They are fast and they are easy, but you won't be cut short on flavor or satisfaction with any of these delicious dinners.

This salad is actually inspired by a dessert! While working for Gualtiero Marchesi in Paris, I was taught to make a simple dessert of shaved fennel, crisped in iced water, then tossed in orange segments, with pistachios sprinkled on top.

You can of course serve the orzo warm, but I prefer it cold. I recommend doubling the recipe, so you can have extra to take to work the next day.

ORZO, FENNEL, ORANGE & FETA SALAD

SERVES 2

1 fennel bulb
8 oz (220 g) dried orzo
2 oranges
3 tablespoons extra virgin olive oil, or to taste
1 teaspoon lemon juice (optional)
3 oz (80 g) feta cheese
3 tablespoons finely chopped pistachio nuts
leaves from 1 bunch of dill, chopped
sea salt

Slice the fennel bulb as finely as you can, ideally using a mandoline, if you have one. Sprinkle with a pinch of salt.

Cook the orzo according to the package instructions, then drain it in a sieve and run under cold running water to cool it rapidly. Drain very well.

Meanwhile, segment the oranges. Sitting one of the fruits on its base, with a sharp knife remove all the skin and pith (the white stuff), curving the knife down the sides as though it were a barrel. Working over a bowl, slice the knife between the membranes on either side of each segment so it falls into the bowl. Repeat to peel and segment the second orange.

Toss the orzo in the extra virgin olive oil to stop it sticking together, then add the orange segments and shaved fennel. Taste for salt and acidity, adding a little lemon juice if you think it's needed.

Spoon into bowls and crumble over your feta, sprinkling the pistachios and dill over the top.

Many years ago, while Ireland was going through the Great Famine, a large part of the population traveled to other countries to make a new life. Some settled with Native Americans and told them of the strife back home. The Choctaw Nation, though they had very little money, sent a huge donation of yellow cornmeal to Ireland, saving many lives. During the Covid pandemic, the Irish government sent funds to two Native American communities that were struggling, in gratitude for their kindness in our time of need. This dish is simple, and in making it, that history is remembered. It's a great quick recipe to scale up and serve from the center of the table.

BALSAMIC SHRIMP WITH CHERRY TOMATOES & CREAMY POLENTA

SERVES 2

FOR THE POLENTA
2½ cups (600 ml) water
1 teaspoon sea salt
3½ oz (100 g) quick-cook polenta
½ cup (50 g) finely grated
　Parmesan cheese, plus more
　(optional) to serve
2 tablespoons salted butter
scant ½ cup (100 g) milk,
　if needed

FOR THE SHRIMP
1 tablespoon vegetable oil
1 garlic clove, halved
10½ oz (300 g) raw shrimp,
　deveined if needed
7 oz (200 g) cherry tomatoes,
　halved
3 tablespoons balsamic vinegar
½ teaspoon sugar
pinch of chile flakes
2 handfuls of spinach, total
　weight about 1¾ oz (50 g)
good extra virgin olive oil,
　to serve (optional)

Bring the measured water and salt to a boil, then whisk in the polenta: it will cook very quickly. Beat in the Parmesan and butter, then taste and see if it needs more salt. Keep it warm over low heat, covering the surface with a sheet of parchment paper to prevent a skin from forming, and stirring it occasionally, while you quickly cook the shrimp.

Get a frying pan hot over high heat. Add the oil and garlic clove, then throw in the shrimp and cherry tomatoes, along with the balsamic, sugar and chile flakes. The shrimp will change color from blue to pink when they are cooked. Take them off the heat and add the spinach, stirring to wilt.

Mix up the polenta once more: if it seems a little dry, add a little bit of milk at a time to loosen it up.

Spoon the polenta into the middle of the plates or bowls, creating little wells in the center of the mounds. Spoon the shrimp on top. Finishing with some Parmesan, and a drizzle of extra virgin olive oil is a nice touch, if you like.

This recipe works extremely well when you're in a hurry but really want something bursting with flavor. I like to eat it with plain boiled rice, or baby potatoes. You'll find curry powder mixes in the supermarket for a reasonable price, considering the number of spices that are usually in them. I like to go for a mild version, as I can then add more heat, depending on who I am cooking for.

COCONUT COD CURRY

FOR THE COD

½ teaspoon sea salt
1 teaspoon mild curry powder
(or see below)
2 × 3½–3¾ oz (100–110 g)
skinless cod fillets

FOR THE SAUCE

14 oz (400 g) can of coconut milk,
or ¾ cup (200 ml) light cream
plus 4 tablespoons
unsweetened shredded
coconut
2 tablespoons mild curry powder,
or to taste (or see below)
½ teaspoon chile flakes, or to
taste, plus more to serve
(optional)
2 garlic cloves, halved or finely
chopped
bunch of cilantro, stalks finely
chopped, leaves kept separate
½ teaspoon sea salt
½ teaspoon sugar, or to taste
juice of ½ lime, or to taste, plus
lime wedges to serve
up to 2 tablespoons all-purpose
flour, if needed

Preheat the oven to 400°F (200°C).

Sprinkle the salt and curry powder evenly over the cod pieces and place them on a baking sheet lined with parchment paper.

Pour the coconut milk, or cream and shredded coconut, into a pot with the curry powder, chile flakes, if using, garlic, cilantro stalks and salt. Don't be afraid to add more curry powder, if you like, though remember you can't take it out, so a guarded hand is good. Bring to a boil, then reduce the heat to a simmer. Taste for salt and adjust as needed, then add the sugar and lime juice, to taste. Remove the garlic halves, if using.

Meanwhile, bake the cod in the hot oven for 8–10 minutes. Check it is cooked by doing the skewer test (see page 113).

The curry sauce should coat the back of a wooden spoon: when you run your finger through it, it should leave a track. If it is too thin, mix the flour in a small bowl with just enough water to make a smooth paste. Gradually add it to the sauce, stirring, until the consistency is as you prefer. When the sauce bubbles, the flour should be cooked.

Serve the cod and curry sauce with boiled rice or baby potatoes and lime wedges, ripping the cilantro leaves over the top. If you want an extra kick, scatter a few more chile flakes over.

Tricks of the Trade

If you want to make your own curry powder, mix together 2 tablespoons each of ground coriander and ground cumin, then blend in 1 tablespoon each of ground turmeric, chile powder (use mild chile powder, if you prefer) and ground ginger.

When we are up against it in the restaurant kitchen, preparing the staff meal is often pushed down the to-do list until it is nearly too late. It is then that we turn to the kitchen staple we call Pasta Ferrari: it's fast and red, and it's always to share with people we love and care about. Because though it is utterly simple in every way, it will still fai battere il cuore: "make your heart race."

PASTA FERRARI

SERVES 2

5½ oz (150 g) dried spaghetti
3 tablespoons extra virgin olive oil, plus 1 tablespoon
2 garlic cloves, halved
½ red chile, finely chopped, or ½ teaspoon chile flakes
14 oz (400 g) can of chopped tomatoes
2 tablespoons tomato paste
½ teaspoon sugar
½ teaspoon sea salt
2 tablespoons finely grated Parmesan cheese, to serve

Prepare the spaghetti according to the package instructions, then drain—reserving a little of its cooking water—and toss it with the 1 tablespoon of olive oil.

Meanwhile, heat a large pot with the 3 tablespoons of olive oil, then add the garlic and cook for 2–5 minutes or until it is only just turning golden-brown (see below).

Add the chile or chile flakes, tomatoes, tomato paste, sugar and salt and bring to a boil. Cook for 5 minutes.

Beat in a little of the pasta cooking water, to give the sauce a silky quality.

Serve, with the Parmesan in a bowl on the side to scatter over the top.

Tricks of the Trade

As the seasons change, garlic can cook quickly or a little more slowly, depending on how much moisture is in the cloves. Because of this, spring "wet" garlic will cook more slowly than dry winter garlic cloves.

What's great about this is that you can prepare it a day before you need it, leave it in the fridge and have it when you get home. It's also a good dish to bring on a picnic, or take for a lunch at work. Making the dressing in a jar also makes it great for traveling. I've kept this version vegetarian, but cooked chicken or shrimp would be a nice addition.

SUMMER BEAN BOWL

4 tablespoons hummus
generous 1 cup (200 g) canned
    mixed beans (drained weight)
½ cucumber, deseeded and cut
    into half moons
7 oz (200 g) cherry tomatoes
    (about 10), halved
½ yellow pepper, chopped
1 carrot, grated
2 small handfuls baby spinach,
    arugula and watercress, or your
    favorite salad leaves, total
    weight about 1½ oz (40 g)
1 teaspoon mixed seeds

FOR MY HOUSE VINAIGRETTE
2 tablespoons extra virgin olive oil
1 tablespoon white wine vinegar
1 teaspoon honey
1 teaspoon Dijon mustard
pinch of sea salt

Place all the vinaigrette ingredients in a jar, seal the lid and shake it well together.

Spoon the hummus into the center of 2 bowls or containers and then arrange all the salad ingredients except the seeds around it, each one separately so they have their own "zones." Sprinkle the seeds on top of it all.

Shake the vinaigrette jar once more to re-emulsify, then pour it over the bean bowl and dig in.

Tricks of the Trade

When you're thinking of making a salad, stop and ask yourself some questions. What will give it texture? How can I add color to the plate? What extra ingredients have I got on hand that will enhance it, such as toasted nuts, crunchy croutons, edible flowers or the beginnings of shooting herbs and greens? All these will create a salad that really catches the eye and sings to the palate.

This is the single most surprising dish I've made at home. I cannot quite believe that there is such a good recipe for which you need zero cooking ability! You will wow anyone with this. Ideally, make it in a pan that has a lid, but if you don't have a lid you can always use a large heatproof plate to cover the pan instead.

I serve this with proper crusty sourdough bread and a simple arugula salad.

SEA BREAM PUTTANESCA

SERVES 2

2 tablespoons extra virgin olive oil, plus 1 teaspoon
1 garlic clove, halved
2 tablespoons capers
10 Kalamata olives, pitted
7 oz (200 g) cherry tomatoes, halved
14 oz (400 g) can of chopped tomatoes
1 tablespoon sugar
½ teaspoon sea salt
2 sea bream fillets or sea bass fillets
leaves from a bunch of parsley
1¾ oz (50 g) arugula

Heat the 2 tablespoons of oil in a frying pan over medium heat. Add the garlic, capers and olives, stir and cook for a few minutes. Add the cherry tomatoes, chopped tomatoes, sugar and salt and let it bubble together.

Add the fish skin side down, place a lid on top (or see recipe introduction) and reduce the heat to low. Cook for 6 minutes. Once it is cooked (see page 113 to test), remove the lid and add the parsley.

Meanwhile, mix the arugula leaves with the 1 teaspoon of oil.

Serve the puttanesca with the arugula salad, with sourdough bread or toast on the side, if you like.

Tricks of the Trade

If you want to make a vegetarian meal with these flavors, I find replacing the fish with vegetables that you know cook quickly—such as asparagus or bok choi—works brilliantly, because the sauce is so versatile. Either version is also great as a pasta sauce.

This is a dish that you can throw together on a summer evening. It eats really well cold, so would make an ideal salad to take on a romantic picnic, along with a nice cold bottle of rosé.

MUSTARD-CRUSTED SALMON & BUTTER BEAN SALAD

SERVES 2

FOR THE SALAD

generous 1 cup (200 g) canned butter beans (drained weight)
2 tablespoons white wine vinegar
½ teaspoon sea salt
¾ cup (100 g) frozen peas, defrosted under running water and drained
1 green zucchini, cut into strips with a vegetable peeler, seedy core discarded
1 tablespoon extra virgin olive oil
1 tablespoon Dijon mustard (optional)
leaves from a bunch of parsley, chopped

FOR THE SALMON

2 tablespoons wholegrain mustard
1 teaspoon honey
juice of ½ lemon
2 salmon fillets, skin on or off, as you prefer
sea salt

In a bowl, combine the butter beans, vinegar and salt. Mix well, then add the peas and zucchini ribbons. Finally, stir in the olive oil, Dijon mustard, if you want to give it a little kick, and parsley.

Preheat the oven to 425°F (220°C).

Mix the wholegrain mustard, honey and lemon juice together in a small bowl with a pinch of salt and smother the salmon fillets in this so they are covered all over. Set them on a small baking sheet, skin side down if you are using fillets with skin. Bake for 10 minutes.

Once the salmon is cooked—check by doing the skewer test (see page 113)—serve it hot or cold on top of the bean salad.

If I go to a supermarket with a fish counter, I always check if they have fresh mussels or cockles. These shellfish grow so well in Irish waters and we really should eat them more. They are easy and quick to prepare and, to be honest, if you just cook them in a splash of white wine or water they are delicious! But if you want to make more of an effort, this recipe is still very easy but worth it. I originally made this pesto with lovage, but that is hard to find these days. Lovage grew in the wild many years ago and was a popular herb, before similar-tasting celery arrived in the seventeenth century and was regarded as a delicacy, sweeping lovage out of its path.

If you want a more substantial meal, add 5½ oz (150 g) sliced boiled baby potatoes and ¼ cup (50 g) sugar snap peas.

MUSSELS WITH HERB PESTO

SERVES 2

¼ garlic clove
½ bunch of tarragon
½ bunch of parsley
pinch of sugar
3½ tablespoons extra virgin
    olive oil
1 lb 5 oz (600 g) mussels
2 celery stalks, peeled and
    chopped
finely grated zest of 1 lemon
sea salt

In the jug of an immersion blender or food processor, mix the garlic, tarragon, parsley, sugar, a pinch of salt and the extra virgin olive oil. Blend until combined (see tip, below).

If any mussels are open, tap them to see if they close. You are checking to see if they are alive, as they will only close if they are. Discard the shells that stay open.

To prepare the mussels, pull off the "beards," which are the hairy strands emerging from the shells and are actually bits of the rope the mussels were grown on. With a small knife, scrape off any barnacles. If any mussels are cracked, discard them. Rinse briefly to remove any debris from the shells.

Place a wide-based pan with a lid over medium heat. Tip in your mussels and celery and cook, gently opening the mussels. (If any mussels refuse to open after 5–8 minutes, discard them.)

Add the herb pesto to the mussel pan and toss until fully coated, then serve steaming hot, sprinkled with the lemon zest.

Tricks of the Trade

When blending in a food processor, think of what the desired texture should be, unlike puréeing (see page 181) when you always want a silky-smooth result. If you are making pesto, as here, you want the ingredients united, but still to have different flecks of color and a nubbly texture. It is a quick process and you have to watch carefully and stop when it is just right.

My restaurant Myrtle is closed on Mondays. Usually, after a weekend, I want to eat something light and on the healthy side, but I never want to spend ages in the kitchen, as I've still got a lot of admin to do while the restaurant is closed. So it has worked out that I make a version of this recipe most Mondays!

MONDAY NIGHT SALMON WITH CHICKPEAS, PEAS & WATERCRESS

SERVES 2

2 × 3½ oz (100 g) salmon fillets, skin on or off, as you prefer
heaped 1 cup (200 g) canned chickpeas (drained weight)
2½ tablespoons extra virgin olive oil
¾ cup (100 g) frozen peas
finely grated zest and juice of 2 lemons
handful of watercress or arugula, 3 oz (80 g) total weight
sea salt and freshly ground black pepper

Preheat the oven to 400°F (200°C).

Season the salmon with salt and pepper and place on a baking sheet. Cook in the oven for 10 minutes. Check it is cooked by doing the skewer test (see page 113).

Meanwhile, pour the chickpeas onto a large plate and crush with a fork.

Put the extra virgin olive oil in a pot with a pinch of salt and add the chickpeas and your frozen peas. Set over low heat and slowly warm up, adding the zest and juice of 1 lemon. Give it a mix and taste to see if it needs more salt (see below).

Take a handful of watercress or arugula and place it in the center of the plates.

Spoon your chickpea and pea mixture over and flake the salmon on top. Add the remaining lemon zest and a squeeze of the juice and you're ready to go.

Tricks of the Trade

Salt is an enhancer of other flavors as well as a flavoring in its own right. So if a small amount goes in at the beginning of cooking anything, it will make each ingredient taste better.

When I was a kid, a "salad" was what we actually called lettuce leaves: any of them were labeled "salad." I'm so amazed at how food at home and in restaurants has evolved over the years! There was a time when people thought salad was boring... for any of you who might still need convincing that is very much not true, this is the salad for you. It is the perfect meal to throw together in 10-20 minutes. If you really are in a hurry, you could slice the chicken more finely and the strips will cook in half the time.

CHICKEN SATAY SALAD

SERVES 2

FOR THE CHICKEN AND MARINADE
½ teaspoon ground cumin
1 garlic clove, crushed
2 tablespoons vegetable oil
½ red chile, finely sliced
½ teaspoon sea salt
2 skinless chicken breasts, each sliced into 3 lengthways

FOR THE SAUCE
1 small onion, finely chopped
½ red chile, finely sliced, plus more to serve
2 tablespoons soy sauce
scant 1 cup (200 ml) coconut milk, stirred to amalgamate
3 tablespoons crunchy peanut butter
½ teaspoon sugar
finely grated zest and juice of 1 lime
sea salt

FOR THE SALAD
2 heads of Baby Gem lettuce, quartered
2 tablespoons mixed chopped nuts
handful of cilantro leaves

Preheat the oven to 400°F (200°C).

In a bowl, mix the cumin, garlic, 1 teaspoon of the oil, the chile and salt. Marinate the chicken breasts in this for 5 minutes, then wipe the marinade off into a saucepan.

Place the chicken on a baking sheet and roast in the oven for 15–20 minutes.

Meanwhile, put the saucepan of marinade over medium heat and add the remaining oil, the onion, chile, soy sauce and coconut milk. Bring to a boil, then stir in the peanut butter and sugar. Taste the sauce and add the lime zest and juice to bring it to life, then season to taste with salt.

Place the lettuce on one side of the plates and the chicken on the other. Pour the sauce on top of the lettuce and scatter with more chile slices, the chopped nuts and cilantro.

Tricks of the Trade

These flavors can be enjoyed hot or cold, so if you have any leftover sauce and chicken, save it in the fridge, add any chopped vegetables you have on hand, and create a new version for the next day's lunch.

My partner Rich has a handful of dishes that he makes for lunches and dinners for us. He hates cooking, not because he's bad at it, but because he doesn't think the extra time spent making a dish more special is worth it. So he only makes dishes that are super-quick, involve minimum cleaning and are still delicious. This was the first recipe I taught him to make. I have lost count of how many times we have had it for dinner and it never disappoints.

FENNEL SAUSAGE MEATBALLS

SERVES 2

8 sausages, skins removed, or
    7 oz (200 g) ground pork
1 tablespoon fennel seeds
3 tablespoons sunflower oil
    or vegetable oil
1 garlic clove, halved
1 onion, finely chopped or grated
½ teaspoon sea salt
½ teaspoon sugar
14 oz (400 g) can of chopped
    tomatoes
1 tablespoon tomato paste
pinch of sugar (optional)
handful of baby spinach
5½ oz (150 g) dried linguine
extra virgin olive oil
Parmesan cheese, to serve

Mix the sausage meat or ground pork in a bowl with the fennel seeds.

Place a large frying pan over medium heat. Add the oil and, using a teaspoon, spoon the sausage or pork mixture onto the hot pan. Leave until the meatballs are golden brown on their bases, then turn over.

Add the garlic, onion, salt, sugar, tomatoes and tomato paste. Bring to a boil, then reduce the heat and simmer for 5–10 minutes. Taste, and see if it needs a sprinkle of sugar, which it might if your canned tomatoes are acidic. Add the spinach and give the mixture a quick stir to wilt the leaves.

Meanwhile, cook the linguine according to the package instructions, then drain it, reserving a little of the cooking water. Return the pasta to its pan and toss it in a little extra virgin olive oil.

Add a spoonful of the pasta cooking water to the sauce and stir it well, then serve the linguine with the meatballs, offering Parmesan to grate over the top.

A great use for leftover mashed potatoes and so easy that I hope it becomes a staple quick meal you can rapidly bring together at home. In the restaurant, when we have a little leftover mash, I quickly throw these together to feed my whole kitchen crew. They are also lovely for breakfast if you've woken up and there's no bread in the house. You can of course remove the bacon and add asparagus spears and maybe some shavings of Parmesan, for a vegetarian version, or even just a poached egg on top.

POTATO CAKES WITH BACON RASHERS & MUSHROOMS

SERVES 4

FOR THE TOPPING
2 tablespoons salted butter
1 garlic clove, halved
8 smoked bacon rashers, snipped
   with scissors into strips, or
   3 oz (80 g) smoked lardons
7 oz (200 g) cremini mushrooms,
   quartered

FOR THE POTATO CAKES
3½ oz (100 g) cold mashed
   potatoes
1⅔ cups (200 g) self-rising flour,
   plus more if needed and to dust
1 egg, lightly beaten
½ teaspoon sea salt
2 tablespoons vegetable oil
leaves from ½ bunch of flat
   leaf parsley
3 oz (80 g) kale, coarse ribs
   removed, leaves finely chopped

FOR THE DRESSING
¼ cup (60 ml) extra virgin olive oil
2 tablespoons balsamic vinegar
pinch of sugar
sea salt

Heat 1½ tablespoons of the butter in a frying pan and add your garlic. Cook for 2 minutes, then add your bacon and cook for 5 minutes. Now add your mushrooms and cook for 5 minutes. Add the remaining ½ tablespoon of butter over low heat, stirring to create an emulsion.

In a bowl, mix the potatoes, flour, egg and salt. You are looking for it to be wetter than scone dough. If it's super-wet it will still work: you can spoon it into the pan like thick batter. Dust your work surface with flour and split your potato mixture into 4 balls. Shape each into a patty. Preheat the oven to 385°F (195°C).

Heat an ovenproof frying pan with the oil and cook the potato cakes for 2–3 minutes until golden brown, then flip and put it into the oven for 5 minutes. If you don't have an ovenproof pan, lift them onto a baking sheet before you put them in the oven.

Meanwhile, mix all the ingredients for the dressing in a bowl with a pinch of salt. Toss the parsley and kale in the dressing and serve with the potato cakes fresh out of the oven, with the mushrooms and bacon.

Tricks of the Trade

Mixing: an important term including stirring, beating or binding with a spoon, creaming with a paddle, whipping with a whisk or folding with a spatula. The two main goals are:

Air: avoiding or encouraging more air into the recipe.

Damage: you either want to cause it—as when beating to break down an ingredient—or prevent it, as you might when folding.

A wonderful light lunch or easy dinner. Ideally you would use eight metal or wooden skewers here to form the meat around, but if you don't have those, shape the koftas into sausage shapes and fry them in a frying pan instead.

LAMB KOFTA WITH YOGURT DRESSING & HERBY CUCUMBER SALAD

MAKES 8 / SERVES 4

FOR THE KOFTAS
14 oz (400 g) ground lamb
1 teaspoon ground cumin
½ teaspoon chile flakes
1 teaspoon dried oregano
1 garlic clove, crushed
1 teaspoon sea salt
1 tablespoon water
4 small pita breads, to serve

FOR THE SALAD
1 cucumber, grated
½ bunch of dill, chopped
leaves from ½ bunch of mint

FOR THE SAUCE
1¼ cups (300 g) thick Greek-style yogurt
2 tablespoons extra virgin olive oil
1 teaspoon white wine vinegar
1 tablespoon fresh white breadcrumbs (optional)
sea salt

Preheat the oven to 410°F (210°C). Put the lamb in a bowl with the spices, oregano, garlic and salt and mix really well with your hands. Just as you think you have combined it enough, mix in the measured water (see below).

Make 8 kofta sausage shapes around metal or wooden skewers (or see recipe introduction), then place on roasting pan and bake for 10 minutes.

Meanwhile, mix together the cucumber, dill and mint in a bowl.

In a second bowl, mix the Greek yogurt with the olive oil and vinegar, seasoning to taste with salt. If your sauce seems a bit loose—which can happen if the yogurt was runny—you might want to add the breadcrumbs to thicken it up.

Put the pita breads in the toaster, then cut in half with scissors. Spoon the cucumber salad onto plates, spoon some of the yogurt dressing over it, then add the koftas. Serve the toasted pitas on the side, for people to stuff as they choose, along with a bowl of the remaining yogurt dressing. Dig in!

Tricks of the Trade

Adding water to any meatball or burger mixture will help to keep it soft and juicy when cooked.

Controversially, I sometimes like a steak with a little chew to it; the chewing adds flavor. Time for a second controversial statement: sometimes filet mignon, to me, tastes bland. If you can give yourself the time to quickly marinate a sirloin steak, that will help to tenderize it and it cooks lickedy-quick. If you want to add a simple sauce, chopped capers mixed into mayo with black pepper works very nicely.

One piece of advice: get the potatoes on first, as they will take 15–20 minutes in the oven. The potato salad is lovely warm or cold, so any left over will not go to waste.

STEAK WITH SPEEDY ROAST NEW POTATO SALAD

SERVES 2

10½ oz (300 g) baby potatoes, halved, or quartered if larger
2–3 tablespoons sunflower oil, plus 1 tablespoon
1 tablespoon honey
1 tablespoon Dijon mustard
½ bunch of chives, finely chopped, or snipped with scissors
2 tomatoes, halved
pinch of sugar
1 × 10½ oz (300 g) sirloin steak, about 1 in (2.5 cm) thick, at room temperature
sea salt and freshly ground black pepper

FOR THE MARINADE
½ teaspoon sweet paprika
1 tablespoon sunflower oil
⅓ teaspoon onion powder
1 tablespoon extra virgin olive oil

Preheat the oven to 400°F (200°C). Place the potatoes on a baking pan. Drizzle with 1–2 tablespoons of oil and add a sprinkle of salt. Roast for 15–20 minutes, or until you can slide a knife easily through them. Mix the honey, mustard and chives together, season with salt and toss the potatoes in it.

Meanwhile, place the tomatoes on a baking pan and sprinkle with salt, the sugar and 1 tablespoon of oil. Roast for 10 minutes.

Mix the marinade ingredients with 10 twists of black pepper and rub all over the steak with a pinch of salt. Set aside for 1–2 minutes while you heat a frying pan over high heat until smoking, with the 1 tablespoon of sunflower oil.

Add the steak and cook for 2 minutes; it should be golden brown. Then turn over and cook for another 2 minutes. Rest on a plate for as long as you can (5 minutes is good). Slice, then serve with the roast potatoes and tomatoes, drizzling the steak resting juices from the plate over the meat.

Tricks of the Trade

Marinating is more useful than you would think. It adds flavor of course, but it also helps to tenderize meat or fish. Even if you only have a couple of minutes, it will help.

Lunch & Brunch

This was a tricky chapter for me to describe to you. It's full of recipes that I really believe to be rewarding and tasty, but which perhaps don't fall into the category of what you'd call a traditional dinner, while some are probably a bit fancy to be called lunch... so I stuck "brunch" in there to help me out a little!

When you think "brunch," you imagine something a little more special than a bit of toast and butter. So this chapter is full of salads, soups, flatbreads and pancakes—most of which would do just fine for the middle of the day—as well as a couple of nicer or more filling options to share with anyone else who might be eating with you.

Included here is my recipe for the perfect Irish soda bread, baked in bean cans, great for dipping in soups or crumbling to make breadcrumbs to toast and scatter over a salad. Or, when it gets a little stale, you can slice it thinly and put it in the oven to make cracker breads.

As with the recipes throughout this book, I've added extra nuggets of information to help you to make them more impressive, without needing a huge amount of effort. You'll find the dishes here perfect for when you want to impress over a midday meal.

This recipe makes two large or four smaller flatbreads. The smaller ones are a good size to freeze, then put in the toaster straight from the freezer to use another day.

If you don't have any self-rising flour, replace the amount in this recipe with all-purpose flour and use 1 tablespoon of baking powder instead of the ½ teaspoon here.

GRILLED ROSEMARY FLATBREADS WITH ROASTED TOMATOES & GOAT CHEESE

SERVES 2, WITH EXTRA FLATBREAD FOR ANOTHER DAY

FOR THE ROASTED TOMATOES
2 tablespoons extra virgin olive oil
2 tablespoons balsamic vinegar
1 garlic clove, sliced
7 oz (200 g) cherry tomatoes
pinch of sugar
sea salt

FOR THE FLATBREADS
2½ cups (300 g) self-rising flour, plus more to dust (or see recipe introduction)
½ teaspoon baking powder (or see recipe introduction)
leaves from 1 rosemary sprig, chopped
1 teaspoon sea salt
1 teaspoon sugar
1¼ cups (300 g) plain yogurt
4 teaspoons extra virgin olive oil, plus more to brush

TO SERVE
2 handfuls of spinach or arugula
3½ oz (100 g) goat cheese

Preheat the oven to 400°F (200°C).

Start with the tomatoes. Pour the oil and balsamic vinegar into an oven dish and add the garlic and cherry tomatoes, sprinkling with the sugar and a pinch of salt. Roast for 10 minutes until the tomatoes are soft and the skins have split. Leave to rest on a heatproof surface, so they can absorb the flavors, while you make your flatbreads.

To make the flatbreads, place the flour, baking powder, rosemary, salt and sugar in a large bowl and mix to combine, then create a well in the center. Add the yogurt and olive oil to the well and mix in the flour until it starts to form into a ball. If the mixture is too dry, add 1 tablespoon of water to bring the dough together. Now give it a very light knead for 1 minute, just to bring it together.

Dust a work surface with flour and divide the dough into 4 pieces. Roll each piece into a circle 6–7 in (16–18 cm) in diameter with a rolling pin. Brush each flatbread with oil. Keep them on a sheet of oiled parchment paper ready to cook. (You can also make the recipe into 2 large flatbreads, if you prefer, though you'll need a pan big enough to cook them in.)

Heat up a griddle or frying pan over high heat until it is very hot. Place a flatbread on the pan and cook for 2 minutes, then turn over, reduce the heat to medium-low and cook for a further 3 minutes. Repeat to cook all the flatbreads (though you only need 2 for this meal).

Brush 2 flatbreads with more extra virgin olive oil and place on plates. Put a handful of spinach or arugula on the 2 flatbreads along with the roasted cherry tomatoes, then crumble the goat cheese over the top to serve.

Anything you want can go into these instead of the spices here: try chile flakes if you like a bit of heat, or just make them plain and scatter them with sea salt flakes.

The dough should be warm at all stages, as that's what makes it elastic; you don't want it to get dry or cold.

PINK PEPPERCORN & CARDAMOM GRISSINI

MAKES ABOUT 30

1 tablespoon (9 g) active dry
    yeast, or ¾ oz (21 g) fresh yeast
2 teaspoons sugar
1½ cups (355 ml) warm water
2½ tablespoons olive oil, plus
    more to knead and roll
4⅓ cups (520 g) strong white
    bread flour
2 teaspoons fine sea salt
1 egg white
1 tablespoon pink peppercorns,
    crushed
seeds from 5 green cardamom
    pods, crushed, or 1 teaspoon
    fennel seeds (optional)
sprinkle of sea salt flakes

Put the yeast and sugar in a bowl (crumble the yeast in, if using fresh). Very gradually add the measured warm water, mixing very well, then cover with a cloth and leave for 5–10 minutes until frothy. Stir in the olive oil.

Mix the flour and salt together in a large bowl. Create a well in the center of the flour, add your yeast liquid, then mix to form a dough. Oil a work surface, then knead the dough on it with the heel of your hand for 5–10 minutes, to exercise the gluten in the flour. This mix is best kept warm, for added stretchiness.

Oil a large bowl and put the dough in, oiling the surface of the dough as well. Cover with a cloth and leave in a warm place until doubled in size, which will take 1–2 hours depending on the temperature of the kitchen and the time of year.

Preheat the oven to 365°F (185°C).

Once it has doubled in size, knock the dough back by giving it a few gentle punches—let that stress out!—and re-knead briefly to remove any air bubbles. Leave it to relax on the work surface for a minute or so, to make it easier to work with.

Oil a work surface and roll out the dough with a rolling pin to a rectangle measuring about 12 x 8 in (30 × 20 cm). Brush with your egg white and go wild with what spices you love. I've chosen pink peppercorns and cardamom or fennel. Whichever spices you choose, you'll also want to sprinkle it with sea salt flakes.

Cut the dough widthways into pieces less than ½ in (1 cm) thick. Pick up a piece and gently shake it, so it stretches with the effect of gravity, then put it on an oiled baking sheet, with the very ends of each grissini hanging over the sides. Repeat to form all the grissini. You should get about 30 sticks.

Bake for 10–15 minutes until golden brown, then leave to cool. These will keep in an airtight continer for weeks.

Growing up, we had fresh brown (soda) bread baked weekly by my Aunt Sadie. She measured the ingredients for it with her hands; she never used a scale. My Granny Donnelly was also a great baker. I remember on Sundays, after mass, going to sit in Granny's kitchen. As my mother and Granny chatted, I stared up to the cookie tin on the shelf, waiting on tenterhooks for the moment Granny would offer whatever baked delights she had in there. With this recipe, I've taken my talented Aunty's guesswork out of baking, and if you follow it, you are sure to be sinking your teeth into delicious homemade bread without any trouble.

The traditional Irish soda bread was literally made from just buttermilk, salt, flour and baking soda, and was best eaten on the day it was baked. I've brought the recipe up to date and added butter, sugar and egg, which makes the crumb softer and allows it to stay fresh for up to three days, so there's less chance that any of it will go to waste. If you keep it in the fridge it will last even longer and be great for toast (though not for sandwiches, if you have chilled it, as that toughens the texture).

A clever way to use leftover cans from your baked beans is to wash them out and use them for this recipe. If you don't have any cans, an 8½ in x 4½ in (1 lb/500 g) loaf pan will do.

BAKED BEAN CAN SODA BREAD

2 tablespoons salted butter, plus more for the cans or pan
2⅔ cup (300 g) coarse wholewheat flour, plus more for the cans or pan
½ teaspoon baking soda
1 teaspoon baking powder
2 tablespoons brown sugar
1 teaspoon fine sea salt
1 egg, lightly beaten
3 cups (700 ml) buttermilk

Preheat your oven to 425°F (220°C). Butter and flour 2 empty bean cans, or an 8½ in x 4½ in (1 lb/500 g) loaf pan. It's important to have your oven preheated and your cans or pan prepared before starting the recipe, as once the dough is mixed it is best baked immediately.

Melt the butter and leave it to cool slightly. Put all the dry ingredients in a large bowl and mix so they are evenly dispersed. Make a well in the center, then add the cooled melted butter to the well with the egg and buttermilk and mix well and quickly with a spoon. Your mixture should be wet and drop off the spoon.

Working fast, divide the dough between the prepared cans or place in the pan. Bake for 10 minutes, then reduce the oven temperature to 350°F (180°C) and cook for a further 35 minutes.

Take the bread out of the cans or pan and let cool. Once cool, if you wrap it in plastic it will stay fresh for longer. This is delicious just with butter, or wonderful with smoked salmon.

Carrots get a bad rep. I mean, where would we be without this humble veg? She fills up salads, Sunday roasts and hummus platters. Not only is she super-affordable, but she is bursting with goodness, she grows fast and plentifully in Ireland and is a vegetable to be celebrated well outside of just a role as filler.

CARROT & CUMIN SOUP

5 large carrots, grated or
    finely chopped
1 tablespoon cumin seeds
1 tablespoon sugar, or to taste
3½ tablespoons heavy cream
3½ tablespoons salted butter
about 1¼ cups (300 ml) vegetable
    stock or water
½–¾ cup (120–175 ml) milk
sea salt

TO SERVE
1 teaspoon salted butter, plus
    1 tablespoon at room
    temperature
3½ oz (100 g) spinach
4 tablespoons chopped
    pecans
1 tablespoon poppy seeds

Put all the ingredients for the soup, except the milk, in a pot with a large pinch of salt; you need enough stock or water to come halfway up the level of the carrots.

Cover and cook over low heat for 15–20 minutes (see below). When you can squash a carrot piece between your thumb and forefinger, it is ready to be blended. Of course, if you like a bit of texture, you don't need to blend it at all. And if you prefer a smooth bowlful, feel free to blend the whole lot.

However, what I do is place half the soup in a blender, add half the milk and blend. Add more milk, if needed, to achieve the consistency you're after.

When the soup is silky-smooth, I return it to the pot with the unblended half. Taste for salt and sugar and add more of either as needed. Reheat until piping hot, but do not bring to a boil.

When ready to serve, melt the 1 teaspoon of butter in a frying pan with a pinch of salt and set over medium-high heat. Add your spinach and cook, stirring, until wilted down.

Rub the 1 tablespoon of butter along the bottom of the bowls, sweeping upwards with a pastry brush or your thumb. Sprinkle the nuts and seeds onto the butter. Place a heaped spoon of spinach in each bowl. Pour in the soup and serve.

Tricks of the Trade

Even though the soup base is cooked over gentle heat here, covering it with a lid means it is ready quickly, and also traps in all the flavors.

Years ago, both my sisters went soup-wild. They talked of nothing else and shared soup recipes constantly. We have all had our own versions of this warm, rich soup. You can put whatever spices you like in it and you can make it with milk, cream or coconut milk as the liquid. This is what makes home cooking so exciting: you get to choose what you think would be most delicious in your own soup.

If parsnips are out of season, the same recipe works really well with the same amount of cauliflower instead.

PARSNIP & ROSEMARY SOUP

1 lb 2 oz (500 g) parsnips
1¼ cups (300 ml) milk, plus
    more if needed
scant ½ cup (100 ml) heavy
    cream
1 teaspoon sea salt, plus more
    if needed
leaves and stalks from 3 rosemary
    sprigs, separated
extra virgin olive oil

Peel the parsnips, cut them in half lengthways, then into quarters. Remove the woody cores from each piece.

Chop the parsnips roughly and put them in a pot with the milk, cream, salt and rosemary stalks. The liquid should come halfway up the level of the parsnips, so add a little more milk if needed.

Cover with a lid and cook over medium-low heat. Check if it's ready after 5 minutes: if you can squash a piece of the parsnip between your finger and forefinger, take it off the heat. If not, cook for a little longer until you can.

Meanwhile, heat a little oil in a frying pan, fry the rosemary leaves until aromatic and crisp, then tip the oil and rosemary from the pan into a small bowl.

When the parsnip is squashable, remove the rosemary stalks from the pot and blend the soup for 3–4 minutes until very silky-smooth. Add more milk if needed to achieve the consistency you prefer, then taste for salt. Reheat until piping hot, but do not bring to a boil.

Serve with a drizzle of the rosemary-infused oil and sprinkled with the fried rosemary leaves, with chunks of crusty bread alongside, if you like.

You could say that my motivation to write this book actually stemmed from this soup! I often spend Christmas with my sister Sarah and her family in Spain, and one year I made them this. Now, my nieces insist this is the only appetizer they want on Christmas Day. The idea that a dish I threw together could be so important to them made me think that, perhaps, writing a cookbook would be good, to pass recipes down through the many children in our family.

On a special day such as Christmas, it's always nice to present food in the least complicated but still elegant manner. I think any home cook could do this dish justice.

CARAMELIZED RUTABAGA & HONEY SOUP

SERVES 4

1 rutabaga (yellow turnip),
   about 14 oz (400 g)
3½ tablespoons salted butter
3 garlic cloves, chopped
2 tablespoons honey, or to taste
2 cups (500 ml) water
2 cups (500 ml) milk
scant ½ cup (100 ml) heavy
   cream
2 tablespoons hazelnuts
2 teaspoons chia seeds
heaped 1 tablespoon black
   sesame seeds
leaves from ½ bunch of parsley,
   chopped
sea salt

Peel and chop the rutabaga. Heat a large pot and add the butter. Fry the rutabaga until golden brown on all sides, then add the garlic and stir for 1 minute. Add the honey and watch it bubble, while still stirring, for 1 minute (see below).

Pour in the measured water and simmer for 10 minutes before adding the milk and cream. Bring to a boil, then reduce the heat to a simmer. Cook until you can squash the rutabaga with the back of a spoon (30–40 minutes).

Preheat the oven to 400°F (200°C). Tip your nuts and seeds onto a baking sheet and place in the oven to toast for 4 minutes. Chop the hazelnuts and let all the nuts and seeds cool.

It's now time to blend the soup. You want it to be as smooth as possible, so a blender is best here (see page 37). Once you have puréed the soup, taste it for salt and the sweetness of the honey and adjust if needed. Reheat the soup gently until just beneath a boil.

Sprinkle the toasted nuts and seeds in the bowls and add the parsley. Ladle the hot soup into the bowls and serve.

Tricks of the Trade

By letting honey bubble and caramelize—here and in other dishes—it both reduces its sweetness and maximizes the flavor.

Christmas Day was the day upon which we kids had the most exquisite treat: the Rule of all Rules could be broken. My parents were very strict about treats and sweets, but, on Christmas Day, we could wake up and devour a whole chocolate selection box for breakfast if we wanted. Then, for our "second breakfast," we had smoked salmon. This was usually around noon, closer to the time when most families ate their main Christmas meal. We never had our actual celebratory dinner until 7 or 8pm... how very Mediterranean of my parents ;)

This recipe shouldn't be saved for a once-a-year treat. It is a birthday breakfast, or a new job lunch. It can be made in advance, so you can take it to work with you and make everyone jealous. If smoked salmon isn't your bag, cold cuts work really well in its place. And there's nothing stopping you from whipping up a batch of pancakes or crêpes just for you, as they freeze excellently (see below).

SMOKED SALMON CRÊPES

MAKES 4

FOR THE CRÊPES
1 cup (120 g) all-purpose flour
1 large egg, lightly beaten
generous ¾ cup (200 g) milk
sea salt (optional)
1 tablespoon sunflower oil,
  or salted butter, for frying

FOR THE FILLING
1 cup (200 g) thick Greek-style
  yogurt or cream cheese
2 tablespoons finely chopped dill,
  plus more to serve
2 teaspoons lemon juice (about
  ½ small lemon), or to taste,
  plus lemon wedges to serve
3½ oz (100 g) smoked salmon,
  cut into strips
sea salt and freshly ground
  black pepper

To make the crêpes, mix the flour and egg in a bowl, then whisk in half of the milk until smooth. Add the remaining milk and whisk until combined. Add a pinch of salt if you are frying these in oil, or leave it out if using salted butter. Pour into a jug and set aside.

For the filling, mix the yogurt or cream cheese, dill and lemon juice with salt and pepper in a bowl. Adjust the seasoning to taste, adding a little extra lemon juice if needed. Set aside.

Brush a little oil or butter over a small nonstick frying pan, no larger than 7 in (18 cm). Pour in one-quarter of the batter and swirl to cover the base. Cook for 1 minute until the base of the pancake is golden brown in places. Loosen the sides with a spatula, then flip. Cook the other side for 40–60 seconds more. Transfer to a warmed plate while you cook the remaining 3 pancakes.

Spread each crêpe with the dill mixture and top with salmon and more dill. Fold or roll them and serve with lemon wedges.

Tricks of the Trade

If you make more pancakes than you need (the batter is easy to scale up), freeze with sheets of parchment paper between each, then use the rest when you feel like it. Anything you can do with bread can be done with a pancake. Use as a sandwich wrap, stuff with chocolate spread and bananas, or bake strips in a hot oven until crispy and use as croutons for salads or soup.

This is a real treat on a summer's day. And it's good to scale up and serve for guests, as everything can be done in advance, except dressing the cucumber and watercress as you are about to serve. If you want to make the meal a bit more filling, some boiled baby potatoes dressed with olive oil, salt and chopped chives served alongside would be perfect.

SALMON STUFFED WITH HORSERADISH, WITH CUCUMBER-WATERCRESS SALAD

SERVES 2

½ cup (100 g) cream cheese
finely grated zest and juice of
    ½ lemon, plus lemon wedges
    to serve
1 tablespoon horseradish sauce
1 cucumber
6 slices of smoked salmon, total
    weight about 4¼ oz (120 g)
4 teaspoons olive oil
1 teaspoon honey
handful of watercress (or
    arugula), total weight
    about 3 oz (80 g)
sea salt

Mix the cream cheese, lemon zest and horseradish together and taste to see if it needs some lemon juice added. Otherwise, keep that for your dressing.

With a vegetable peeler, peel strips all the way down the cucumber lengthways until you get to the seeds, then stop, turn the cucumber around and repeat until you are just left with the center seeds. Discard those.

Cut your smoked salmon slices in half lengthways to create strips. Lay them on a board.

Divide blobs of your cream cheese mix towards one end of each smoked salmon strip, then roll them up gently, so you don't disturb the filling. Turn over so the parcels are seam-side down.

Put your olive oil and remaining lemon juice in a small bowl and add the honey and a pinch of salt to create a zingy dressing. Spoon this over your watercress (or arugula) and cucumber. Serve straight away with the salmon parcels and lemon wedges.

Tricks of the Trade

This recipe works really well if you use the shaved ribbons of cucumber flesh (not any bits with seeds) instead of the smoked salmon, for a vegetarian version.

I always sing my mother's praises to the high heaven regarding her cooking and home economic skills… but this time I have to say that even the greatest cooks have their Achilles heel. And liver was hers. Whenever she'd make it, she would always be sure to mention its nutritional value, in response to which eight little eyes would roll to the top of their heads with dread. She only cooked lamb's liver. Or rather overcooked it. Large pieces would drag down my throat because I tried not to chew them much— not unlike a snake tackling an egg—so I could make it all disappear as quickly as possible.

But putting that aside, I'm going to show you a simple easy recipe—yes, bursting with nutrition!—that I promise won't make you roll your eyes. Or do a snake impression.

PAN-FRIED CHICKEN LIVERS WITH CAPERS ON TOAST

SERVES 2

7 oz (200 g) chicken livers
2 tablespoons vegetable oil
2 tablespoons capers
2 thick slices of sourdough
2 tablespoons white wine, or chicken stock
2¾ tablespoons salted butter
handful of parsley leaves, plus more to serve
sea salt and freshly ground black pepper

Take your chicken livers out of the package and pat them dry on paper towels. Season with salt and pepper.

Heat up a frying pan, pour in your oil and add your chicken livers. After 2 minutes, turn the livers over and add your capers. Cook for 1 minute.

Meanwhile, toast the sourdough slices.

Now add your wine or stock to the livers and take the pan off the heat. Stir in your butter to emulsify and finish with the parsley. Taste and adjust the seasoning. Serve the livers on the toasted sourdough with more parsley sprinkled on top.

Tricks of the Trade

If you have time, try soaking the livers in a small bowl of milk for a few minutes before cooking. It both tenderizes the livers and helps to purify them.

I created this recipe while filming Ready Steady Cook. *With my heart in my mouth, I zoomed around that kitchen and unwittingly invented a go-to snack or dinner that I now regularly turn to at home.*

Seeds are full of fiber and very good for your gut, so the coating has more health benefits than just using the regular breadcrumbs.

SEEDED CHICKEN NUGGETS

FOR THE COATING
3 tablespoons white sesame seeds
3 tablespoons black sesame seeds
1 tablespoon nigella seeds
⅔ cup (100 g) quick-cook polenta cornmeal

FOR THE NUGGETS
2 boneless skinless chicken breasts, or 4 boneless skinless chicken thighs
¼ teaspoon sea salt, plus more for sprinkling
1 egg yolk
scant ½ cup (100 ml) heavy cream
sunflower oil
freshly ground black pepper

FOR THE RED PEPPER MAYO DIP
1 red pepper, deseeded and chopped
1 red chile, deseeded if you like, then chopped
1 small ripe tomato, chopped
1 tablespoon tomato paste
2 teaspoons white wine vinegar
1 egg yolk
½ teaspoon sugar
scant 1 cup (200 ml) sunflower oil

To make the coating, mix the seeds in a bowl with the polenta and place on a biggish tray.

To make the chicken nuggets, take the chicken, scrape away any sinew and cut away any fat or veins. Cut the chicken into chunks and sprinkle with the salt, then place the chicken in a food processor and blend to a paste. Add the egg yolk and a little pepper and pulse-blend to mix. Turn the processor to a low setting and slowly pour in the cream.

Scoop up 1 heaped teaspoon of the chicken mixture and push it off the spoon with your finger onto the tray of polenta and seeds. You should get roughly 16. Sprinkle the seed mixture on top of the nuggets so you cover the chicken completely. Place in the fridge for 30 minutes while you make the dip.

Put the pepper, chile, tomato, tomato paste, vinegar, egg yolk and sugar into a blender and purée until quite smooth on a low speed (see page 37). Slowly pour the oil into it, while blending, until the dip is emulsified and thick.

Back to the nuggets. Pour enough oil into a broad frying pan to cover the base by about ½ in (1 cm), then place it over medium-high heat to heat up for 2–3 minutes. (Throw in a piece of bread: when it sizzles and turns brown, the oil is ready.) Place in the nuggets with a spoon and cook for 3–5 minutes on each side side until golden brown. Drain on paper towels.

Serve in a bowl to share, with the red pepper mayo dip.

Tricks of the Trade

You don't have to fry these bad boys. They will bake very well in just 10 minutes, arranged on a baking sheet and drizzled with oil, in an oven preheated to 400°F (200°C).

Right: couscous doesn't always get people excited, but this might.

My partner Rich was taking part in a Weight Loss Challenge with two of his pals: Lee and Ian. So I created some batch-cooked recipes we could make in bulk, freeze, then defrost in individual portions to suit ourselves. This couscous was my favorite. We named it after the challenge, as we were both so satisfied with the results: it worked for weight loss and is delicious!

As I type, Rich is digging into a bowl and the smell is incredible: the fennel and cumin seeds perfume the air and I can't help but feel happy that I created something healthy, delicious and filling.

RICH'S "WLC" COUSCOUS

MAKES 8 GENEROUS PORTIONS, BUT FREEZES WELL

3 skinless chicken breasts, cut into small bite-sized pieces
4 tablespoons vegetable oil
2 garlic cloves, finely chopped
2 tablespoons cumin seeds
3 tablespoons fennel seeds
1 tablespoon chile flakes
2 onions, finely chopped or grated
3 large carrots, finely chopped or grated
2 red peppers, deseeded and chopped
⅔ cup (100 g) capers
2¼ cups (400 g) dried couscous
1¼ cups (300 ml) boiling water
3–5 tablespoons red wine vinegar
4 tablespoons extra virgin olive oil
heaped 1 cup (150 g) frozen peas, thawed
1 cup (150 g) frozen or canned corn kernels, thawed or drained
sea salt

Sprinkle a little salt over the chicken pieces.

Pour the oil into a large frying pan and add your garlic and a pinch of salt. When the garlic is turning brown, stir in your spices and then your onions. Cook, stirring, until the onions are sweet and soft enough to squash between your fingers. Add the chicken and cook for 7 minutes more over low heat. Now add the carrots, red peppers and capers, stir, then cook for about 5 minutes over low heat.

Weigh out your couscous into a large bowl—there's so much food here that you could even consider using a clean washing-up basin—and pour in the measured boiling water. Leave for a minute, then stir.

Add the red wine vinegar and the olive oil, with 3 teaspoons more salt (this amount of couscous needs it).

Add your cooked veggies, the peas, sweetcorn and chicken to the couscous, stir well, then it's ready to eat, or bag up in portions to freeze.

Tricks of the Trade

This takes only 20 minutes to make a huge amount and we then freeze it in portions. Take a portion out of the freezer the night before you need it and leave in the fridge to defrost, then eat it hot or cold for lunch.

For me, this is the ultimate fancy, celebratory brunch that I was introduced to when I first discovered the meal. Back then, chorizo could be dry and shrivelled because you could only find dry-cured, but now we can easily buy juicy sausages ready for cooking.

If you are using eggs straight from the fridge, just warm them up in tap water for five or ten minutes. This stops the shells from sticking to the eggs when you come to peel them.

This topping is also great with flatbreads (see page 52), if you haven't got any bread in the house.

ROASTED ASPARAGUS WITH BOILED EGGS & FRIED CHORIZO

SERVES 2

2 eggs, at room temperature (see recipe introduction)
1 cooking chorizo *picante* (hot) sausage, sliced
bunch of asparagus, trimmed (see below)
1¾ oz (50 g) kale, coarse ribs removed, leaves chopped
2 thick slices of sourdough
2 heaped tablespoons thick Greek-style yogurt
2 tablespoons chopped parsley leaves
chile flakes, or about ½ red chile, very finely sliced, to serve (optional)
sea salt

Bring a small saucepan of water to a boil. Gently add your room-temperature eggs, using a spoon to place them in the boiling water, and set a timer for 6½ minutes. Once cooked, quickly dip the eggs in cold water, tap all around the shells and peel them off. The eggs will stay warm as long as you do not leave them in the cold water.

Gently fry the chorizo in a frying pan until its own oil is released and it starts to crisp up. Add your asparagus spears to the chorizo and fry for 2 minutes, then add the kale to the pan and cook for another 2 minutes, until wilted.

Meanwhile, toast the sourdough slices. Cut the eggs in half and sprinkle with a little salt.

Spread each slice of toast with the Greek yogurt and place on warmed plates. Top with the asparagus, chorizo, kale and eggs and scatter with the parsley. A few chile flakes or chile slices add a nice kick, if you like.

Tricks of the Trade

When you try to bend an asparagus spear (fresh spears will be brittle), it will snap at the point where it becomes tough. Use just the tender parts in recipes.

"Boxty on the griddle, boxty on the pan. If you can't make boxty, you'll never get a man."

There are so many crossovers in Irish cuisine. We lay claim to quite a few pancakes, some fluffy, others thin and slightly crispy like a French crêpe; these are the latter type. One piece of advice I would give you is this: as soon as you've grated your raw potato, make the mixture and cook it straight away, as we do below.

Boxty come in three forms in Ireland: as a pancake, a boiled dumpling, or a bread similar to a scone. The common thread between them all is that they are made with both cooked and raw potatoes. I'd imagine they were developed to make use of what you had on hand and make sure nothing went to waste. You can easily double this recipe, if you have more potato to use up.

Boxty goes great with poached eggs, or flaked hot-smoked trout. I've put it here with shredded ham hock (pork knuckle) and chive crème fraîche: I love the saltiness and the cool cream alongside the hot crisp pancake.

BOXTY PANCAKES WITH HAM HOCK & CHIVE CRÈME FRAÎCHE

Rinse the grated potato if needed (see below right), drain well, then pat the gratings dry with a clean tea towel. Tip them into a bowl and mix in some salt. The salt will soften the grated raw potato, so the shreds cook quickly with the pancake in the pan.

Put your cold mashed potato, egg, grated potato, flour, the ½ teaspoon of salt and the baking powder into a bowl and mix well with your hands. (They are the best tools for dispersing the mash through the raw grated potato, but you can use a spoon if you prefer.) Mix your milk and lemon juice together, then stir it into the bowl.

You should now have a boxty batter with a thick yogurt-type consistency. The more liquid you add to the batter, the thinner and crisper your boxty will be, which is a style I find lighter and nice in the warmer seasons. If you would like a thicker style of pancake, which can be a welcome treat in the winter, the batter will need a little more flour added to it.

FOR THE BOXTY

5½ oz (150 g) raw potato, peeled
    and grated
½ teaspoon sea salt, plus
    more for the grated potato
3½ oz (100 g) cold mashed potato
1 egg, lightly beaten
generous ¾ cup (100 g) self-
    rising flour, plus more if needed
½ teaspoon baking powder
scant ½ cup (100 ml) whole milk
juice of ½ lemon
vegetable oil

FOR THE TOPPING

2 tablespoons crème fraîche,
    or good-quality thick
    Greek-style yogurt
3½ oz (100 g) shredded ham
    hock, or good-quality ham,
    rolled up and sliced, to give a
    shredded effect
½ bunch of chives, sliced or
    snipped with scissors
handful of arugula

Heat a large frying pan over medium heat with a little vegetable oil. Pour a ladle of your boxty batter on top, reduce the heat under the pan to low and cook until the pancake is golden on the base, then flip it over. You should be able to fit about 4 boxty in the pan at once, depending on its size (and on the size of your boxty). Keep them warm while you continue to cook the rest.

Repeat to make another batch, to cook all the batter. Work quickly, as the boxty are really at their best eaten hot and fresh out of the pan.

Place your boxty on a plate, spread with the crème fraîche or yogurt, evenly sprinkle over the ham hock or shredded ham and finish with a scattering of the chives and arugula.

Tricks of the Trade

Depending on the time of year, I wash grated potatoes. During the old crop season, which runs from September to December in the northern hemisphere, the potatoes are in great shape, their starch is strong and white and they won't need rinsing. Come springtime, the potato starches tend to be converting into sugars and often turn brown or grey quickly. Rinsing these springtime spuds will reduce the extent of that.

Toasties (toasted sandwiches) are a staple in Dublin pubs; Grogan's and O'Donoghue's are especially famous for them. Serving them in a bar is a handy trick to keep people sinking pints of the black stuff! This toastie is a meal in itself. I first created it when I worked in Jersey, after finishing my school Leaving Cert in Dublin. I was always a huge fan of toasted sandwiches anyway, but when you cook them in a frying pan they just become next level. If you want a slightly smaller version, use just two slices of bread and reduce the rest of the recipe by half.

ULTIMATE CHEESE & HAM DOUBLE DECKER TOASTIE

MAKES 1

1 tablespoon olive oil, plus
    2 teaspoons (optional)
1 banana shallot, sliced
3 slices of bread
1 tablespoon Dijon mustard
1¾ oz (50 g) Cheddar cheese,
    grated
2 slices of ham
1 oz (30 g) Taleggio cheese,
    finely sliced
1 oz (30 g) mozzarella cheese,
    finely sliced
2 teaspoons salted butter, at
    room temperature (optional)
sea salt

First thing, get your shallot cooking. Heat up a small pan, add the 1 tablespoon of oil and then the shallot and a pinch of salt. Stir it over medium heat until it starts to turn golden brown. Once that is done, you're ready to build your toastie.

Preheat the oven to 400°F (200°C).

Place the 3 slices of bread on your work surface and spread mustard on each slice. On the first slice, place your Cheddar cheese and ham. Place another slice on top of that, mustard side down. Put your caramelized shallots on top along with your Taleggio and mozzarella cheeses. Place the third slice of bread, again mustard side down, on top of this.

Butter or oil the top of the toastie and place in a cold frying pan, buttered or oiled side down. Now butter or oil the side that is facing upwards. Turn the heat under the pan to medium-low and cook, turning every 2 minutes, until the sandwich gradually turns golden brown and the cheese has melted in the center.

Put the toastie on a baking sheet and put it into the oven for 10 minutes (this is especially useful if you are making a few at the same time), then use the skewer test (see page 113). If the skewer comes out cold, or just warm, give the toastie another 2 minutes in the oven. If it's hot, it's ready to go. Eat straight away.

Veggies

I love vegetables and wish that I could grow them, but alas, every plant I try to nurture I end up somehow killing. I am a serial plant murderer and it breaks my heart. The only thing that makes me feel better about it is that I know what to do once I get my hands on those vegetables that someone else more green-fingered has grown!

When I say I love vegetables, I'm not only talking about fancy Mexican avocados or sweet, ripe Italian tomatoes. They are easy to love and I do. But I also love proper crunchy, sweet, raw carrots; I love the thick chewy-crunchy brown skins on baked potatoes in winter; I love it when spring comes around and everything I want to eat is the color green, from the new broccoli spears to garlic scapes, the young stalks of garlic plants.

As a chef, I've learned how to turn a humble parsnip into a hero ingredient absolutely to be celebrated (read on if you want to do the same) and that is what this chapter is all about: it's my hymn in praise of those wonderful vegetables, often ignored, that we have at our fingertips.

When I first came to London for work, about twenty years ago, as with most people starting out I wasn't paid a lot of money. I often found myself in the supermarket with about £1.20 (about $1.50) to buy dinner for two people: me and my fella. Back then, £1.20 got you a lot more food, of course, but this recipe was (and remains) excellent to make on a tight budget.

There should be enough of this sauce to give you leftovers, which make an amazing toasted sandwich filler.

LENTIL RAGÙ

SERVES 5

FOR THE SAUCE
2 tablespoons vegetable oil,
  or salted butter
2 garlic cloves, finely chopped
1 red chile, finely chopped, seeds
  left in if you want it spicy
1 tablespoon cumin seeds
1 large onion, finely chopped
  or grated
1 thyme sprig
7 oz (200 g) mushrooms,
  chopped
1 carrot, finely chopped or grated
1 celery stalk, finely chopped
scant ½ cup (100 ml) red wine
2 × 14 oz (400 g) cans of
  tomatoes
3 tablespoons tomato paste
4–6 tablespoons vegetarian
  Worcestershire sauce
1 teaspoon sea salt, or to taste
2 teaspoons sugar, or to taste
2 × 14 oz (400 g) cans of brown
  or green lentils, drained
scant ½ cup (100 ml) heavy
  cream

TO SERVE
1 lb 2 oz (500 g) dried spaghetti
1 tablespoon extra virgin olive oil
finely grated vegetarian
  Parmesan cheese
ripped basil leaves (optional)

Set a pot over medium heat, then put in your oil or butter, garlic, chile, cumin seeds, onion and thyme sprig and cook until the onion is sweet and soft. Add the mushrooms and continue to cook out for 10 minutes, to draw out their water. Add the carrot and celery and give it a stir.

Pour in your red wine and let the mix bubble until all the liquid cooks off. Then add the cans of tomatoes, the tomato paste, Worcestershire sauce, salt and sugar and cook, stirring occasionally, for 10–15 minutes.

When the vegetables are soft, add the lentils and cream and bring the sauce to a boil. Taste for salt and sweetness and add more salt or sugar, if you think the sauce needs them.

Cooking dried pasta can be confusing, as it always looks like such a small amount when dry, but trust me, 3–3½ oz (90–100 g) of spaghetti is more than enough for each serving.

Bring a large pot of salted water to a boil. Add your spaghetti and return to a boil, stirring with a large wooden spoon so the spaghetti does not stick together. Cook for 8 minutes, then drain, reserving some of the cooking water. Return the pasta to its pot and toss it in the olive oil both to stop the pasta strands sticking together and to give it a nice flavor.

Quickly add a ladle of pasta cooking water to the lentil sauce and beat it in: this gives it a silky quality.

Using tongs, lift the pasta and place it in the pot of tomatoey lentil ragù. Serve up, scattered with grated cheese and ripped basil leaves, if you like.

I created these for a guest who I hadn't realized was vegetarian. When I found out, I looked in my pantry and pretty much all I had was a bag of frozen peas and some cheese! It didn't look like a meal, but when I put it together it turned into a burger.

These are completely delicious: not only satisfying in flavor, but the texture of the seeds, the spicy horseradish kick and the sweet peas all really complement each other.

PEA & CHEDDAR BURGERS

MAKES 4–6

scant 1 cup (150 g) canned butter
 beans (drained measure)
1½ cups (200 g) frozen peas,
 defrosted
1 egg
1 tablespoon poppy seeds
1 tablespoon sunflower seeds
2 heaped tablespoons
 self-rising flour
½ cup (60 g) grated mature
 Cheddar cheese
vegetable oil
sea salt and freshly ground
 black pepper

TO SERVE
bread rolls (I used *blaa* rolls for
 the photo, traditional in Ireland)
horseradish sauce
sliced tomato
lettuce leaves

Tip the drained butter beans into a large bowl and mash with the end of a rolling pin. Tip in the defrosted peas and do the same. Season the mixture.

Crack the egg into the mashed pea and bean mixture, add the poppy seeds and sunflower seeds and mix well.

Stir in the flour, season again with salt and pepper, then add the cheese and give the mixture a good final mix.

Heat up a dash of oil in a frying pan, then, using a tablespoon, spoon a big dollop of the bean mixture into the hot pan. Depending on how big you have formed them, this recipe should make 4–6 patties.

While the patties are cooking, build your burger bun. Cut the bread rolls in half and dollop on some horseradish sauce straight out of the jar. Pile on the sliced tomato and lettuce.

Keep checking the burgers, flipping, until golden brown on both sides. Use a spatula to transfer out of the pan straight into the bun, then serve.

This is a great recipe to use up your banana skins. Yes, really. Don't worry, you don't have to make your family eat ten bananas in a day! I collected banana skins over three days and then made this dish with them. We are more aware of food waste these days and often want to buy less and act in a more sustainable way with food. Bananas are the most affordable fruit you can buy and are a firm favorite with most children. The skins are packed with fiber (something we all need in our diet every day), potassium and magnesium, which are both good for helping you to maintain good blood pressure. Once you have made this dish, you'll see that you can use banana skins in many recipes, adding them, chopped, to veggie or meat shepherd's pie, for example.

Anyway, I think you might be shocked by both the simplicity and the cost savings you'll get from this recipe.

NO-WASTE VEGAN PULLED PORK WITH SLAW

Start with the slaw. Grate the cabbage and place in a large mixing bowl. In a separate small bowl, mix together the chile and salt, then zest the lime straight into the bowl and add its juice, too. Stir in the sugar or honey until it dissolves into the mixture, then stir this dressing through the shredded cabbage. Cover and set aside, stirring occasionally to redistribute the dressing.

Open a banana skin and, using the tip of a spoon, scrape out the pith, which is the white inside of the skin. This is bitter and has to be scraped away, but it's easily done with a couple of robust scrapes. Repeat to remove the pith from all the bananas.

Now take a fork and scrape the cleaned banana skins very hard in lengthways strokes, hard enough to result in shredding the skins. Put the shredded banana skins into a bowl, discarding the tough end pieces.

In a separate bowl, stir together the cumin, smoked paprika, chile flakes or chile, garlic and a pinch of salt. Mix well with the banana skins so the spices coat all the shreds, then leave to marinate for 5 minutes.

FOR THE SLAW

½ sweetheart cabbage
½ teaspoon chile flakes, or
    ½ red chile, finely chopped
½ teaspoon sea salt
1 lime
½ teaspoon sugar, or honey

FOR THE VEGETARIAN "PORK"

10 large banana skins (see page
    223 for a good recipe for the
    bananas themselves)
1 teaspoon ground cumin
½ teaspoon smoked paprika
½ teaspoon chile flakes, or
    ½ red chile, finely chopped
1 garlic clove, crushed
1 tablespoon vegetable oil
¼ cup (60 ml) water
scant ½ cup (100 ml) barbecue
    sauce
sea salt

TO SERVE

4 large spoonfuls of thick
    Greek-style yogurt or
    mayonnaise
4 burger buns or hot dog buns
leaves from a bunch of cilantro

Warm a large frying pan with the vegetable oil, then add the pulled spiced banana skins and fry them for 2–5 minutes. You just want to make sure the flavorings are cooked at this stage and not raw-tasting.

Add the measured water and continue to cook over medium heat. Take a shred of skin and bite it to check the consistency: you'll know it's tender enough if you like the texture, you're the boss here. If it's ready, stir through the barbecue sauce. Allow the pulled skins to cook and bubble in the barbecue sauce for 1–2 minutes.

Then you're ready to build your burger. Start with putting a dollop of yogurt or mayonnaise on your bun or roll, then pile on your slaw, then add your vegetarian pulled "pork," an extra dollop of yogurt or mayo, some chopped cilantro and more slaw, if you like.

Place on the top of the bun and dig in.

When you think of shepherd's pie you get a warming feeling, which is wonderful when the weather is a bit on the cold side. The dish, in all its forms, offers the relief of a comfort food, and it's often shared. So why not create that same feeling, but without the meat? This is bursting with flavor and really nutritious, and the lentils and mushrooms together give a texture and appearance similar to that of ground meat. You must cook the mushrooms long and slow, to remove their moisture.

MUSHROOM & LENTIL SHEPHERD'S PIE

SERVES 4–5

FOR THE TOPPING
2 lb (900 g) peeled potatoes
3½ tablespoons butter
1 sweet potato, grated
generous ¾ cup (200 g) milk
sea salt and freshly ground
  black pepper

FOR THE FILLING
3–4 tablespoons vegetable oil
4 garlic cloves, finely chopped
small bunch of thyme
2 large onions, finely chopped
  or grated
7 oz (200 g) mushrooms,
  chopped
3 carrots, finely chopped
  or grated
3 celery stalks, finely chopped
¾ cup (175 ml) red wine
3 tablespoons tomato paste
14 oz (400 g) can of chopped
  tomatoes
2 tablespoons cornstarch
  (optional)
1½ cups (300 g) cooked lentils
  (I use Puy lentils, but brown
  lentils or even kidney beans
  are also good)
heaped 1 cup (150 g) frozen peas
sugar

Put the regular potatoes in a saucepan of water, add salt and set over high heat. When they are tender enough that you can slide a knife in, drain the potatoes, then return them to the pan, add the butter and mash. Add the grated sweet potato.

Warm the milk in the microwave or a little saucepan. Add the warm milk to the potatoes gradually, beating, until you have a nice light mash (see below). Taste and add extra salt if needed.

For the filling, heat the oil in a deep pan, add the garlic and, when it has lightly browned, add the thyme and onions. Cook until sweet and golden brown, then add your mushrooms. Cook for 10 minutes, stirring, to draw out the water. Tip in the carrots and celery and cook quickly to soften. Pour in the wine, tomato paste and tomatoes and cook for 30 minutes. If it looks a little wet, in a bowl, mix the cornstarch with just enough water to form a paste and add it gradually, stirring, until the sauce coats the back of a spoon. Mix in the lentils and peas, then taste and adjust with salt and sugar as needed. Pour into a serving dish and—ideally—chill in the fridge. This makes it easier to top with the mash, otherwise that process will be a little messy.

Once your mash is on top, add lots of pepper and keep in the fridge until you are ready to cook. This stays good for 3 days.

Preheat the oven to 400°F (200°C). Cook the pie in the oven for 35–45 minutes. You'll know when it's ready, as the top will be golden brown and the sauce bubbling around the sides. Or use the skewer test (see page 113).

Tricks of the Trade

Using warmed milk and hot potatoes stops those tiny lumps from forming that can make your mashed potatoes grainy.

Sometimes it gets to the end of the month and you want those pennies to stretch further. Recipes such as this will give a great sense of home economy, since you'll save both money and time. Who says fast food can't be healthy? If you don't have onion powder, leave it out, or chop a few chives and add those instead.

KIDNEY BEAN "MEATBALLS" WITH POMODORO SAUCE

SERVES 2 GENEROUSLY

FOR THE SAUCE
8 tomatoes on the vine
2 tablespoons tomato paste
3 garlic cloves
1 onion, chopped
2 tablespoons extra virgin olive oil
pinch of sugar
3 tablespoons chopped oregano
   leaves, or basil or parsley
   leaves, plus more to serve
sea salt and freshly ground
   black pepper

FOR THE "MEATBALLS"
14 oz (400 g) can of red kidney
   beans, drained
½ cup (50 g) fresh white
   breadcrumbs, or crushed
   crackers
1 garlic clove, crushed
½ teaspoon onion powder
   (or see recipe introduction)
1 large egg yolk
generous pinch of cayenne
   pepper
1–2 tablespoons extra virgin
   olive oil
finely grated Parmesan cheese,
   to serve (optional)

Crusty bread or cooked pasta, to
   serve (optional)

For the sauce, put the tomatoes, tomato paste, 2 of the garlic cloves and onion into a food processor or blender and blend.

Put the oil in a Dutch oven or heavy pot over medium heat and add the remaining garlic clove, halved. When it is golden brown, add your blended tomato mix, bring to a boil, then add salt and the sugar. Cook the sauce for 5–10 minutes, stirring regularly.

Add the oregano or other herbs and leave the sauce to simmer gently while you make your meatballs.

Tip half the kidney beans into the cleaned food processor. Add the breadcrumbs or crushed crackers, garlic, onion powder, egg yolk and cayenne pepper and blend with a little pepper until the mixture comes together, adding ½ teaspoon of salt. Don't allow it to become too smooth, as the meatballs need some texture. Place the other half of the beans on a plate and crush them with a fork, then mix them into the blended mixture.

Take 1 teaspoon of mix and push with your finger onto a plate. You should get 25–30 meatballs.

Heat 1 tablespoon of the oil in a large nonstick frying pan and add your kidney bean meatballs. Fry for 5–6 minutes over medium-low heat, turning once, until lightly browned on each side. Add a little more oil if needed.

Gently put the browned meatballs into the sauce, turn to coat them and simmer together for 1–2 minutes more, stirring and adding a splash of water (ideally pasta cooking water, if you're serving this with pasta) to loosen the sauce if needed. Taste and adjust the seasoning. Sprinkle with extra herbs and serve the meatballs with crusty bread, or a nice bowl of pasta and grated Parmesan.

My niece Eliza arrived into this world instinctively loving good food. When she was a very little girl, she used to ask me for a "moo cheese sandwich," by which she meant any stinky cheese that was in my fridge, Camembert and goat cheese included!

Eliza had somehow heard of this recipe and wanted to try it, so she asked her mom—my sister Sarah—if I knew how to make it. I did not, but it sounded great, so I went to the supermarket for some super-large pasta shells. As it turned out, on that day I couldn't get those, though I did find the small ones. I really doubted whether the recipe would work in small pasta shells, but in fact it turned out a treat! I have since made it with jumbo pasta shells, tubes, or even with rigatoni. Basically, any pasta that can be stuffed will work.

One tip I would recommend would be to use a pastry bag: the results are visually pleasing and it saves a lot of time too.

ELIZA'S PASTA

SERVES 4

FOR THE SAUCE
2½ tablespoons vegetable oil
2 garlic cloves, halved
½ teaspoon sea salt
1 oregano sprig
2 red peppers, deseeded
  and chopped
½ red chile, finely chopped
6 ripe plum tomatoes, chopped
4 tablespoons tomato paste
¾ cup (200 g) tomato passata
  or sauce
1 teaspoon sugar (optional)

FOR THE PASTA
10½ oz (300 g) dried large
  conchiglie pasta shells, about
  4 for each person (or see recipe
  introduction)
generous 1 cup (250 g) ricotta
  cheese
1 oz (30 g) Parmesan cheese,
  finely grated, plus more to serve
1 tablespoon chopped oregano
  leaves
sea salt and freshly cracked
  black pepper

First get your sauce on. Put the oil in a wide-bottomed pan and place over medium-low heat. Add your garlic and salt, then the oregano, red peppers, chile, tomatoes and tomato paste, Stir well, then add the passata. Leave this to simmer over low heat for 15 minutes while you get your pasta ready.

Add 1 teaspoon of salt to a large pot of water and cook your pasta shells for 2 minutes less than it says on the package. Drain, then run them under cold water to stop the residual heat from cooking them further (see page 201).

Preheat the oven to 400°F (200°C).

In a bowl, mix the ricotta, Parmesan, chopped oregano and some salt and pepper. Stuff each pasta shell with this mix (this is easier if you use a pastry bag).

Taste the red pepper sauce and add the sugar, if needed. Pour the sauce into an ovenproof dish and nuzzle in the stuffed pasta shells so they are all cheese-side up and the sauce comes up close to their tops. Bake in the oven for 20 minutes.

Scatter straight away with extra Parmesan while the pasta is still in the dish, then serve. This is good on a bed of spinach.

I first relied on this dish when I was living away from home for the first time, in Paris, and existing on a super-tight budget... but that doesn't mean that the recipe is in any way tight on flavor.

Listen, this is a big aul' pot of goodness. The reason I've chosen to put it in this book is that sometimes—when you have a lot of people coming over—you want to make a huge batch of something amazing, but which doesn't take hours to prep and cook. This is it. You could of course add chicken pieces or even shrimp at the end—you're the boss in your kitchen—but I like it vegetarian.

The 6 tablespoons of cumin seeds is not a misprint. This is a lot of food, and the recipe warrants it all. And the lime is a key flavor here: it gives the dish a really fresh sophistication... the oils of citrus fruits are so enticing. Add a sprinkling of lime zest on the top when you serve it, too, if you like.

SPICED THREE BEAN (& CHICKPEA) RAGÙ

SERVES 8-10

3 tablespoons extra virgin olive oil
2 garlic cloves, finely sliced
6 tablespoons cumin seeds, toasted
2 red chiles, finely chopped
3 tablespoons tomato paste
2 × 14 oz (400 g) cans of tomatoes
2 cups (500 ml) vegetable stock
bunch of cilantro, stalks and leaves separated, stalks finely chopped
2 tablespoons sea salt, or to taste
7 oz (200 g) runner beans, trimmed and chopped into diamonds
3 limes, zest peeled off with a vegetable peeler, then juiced
3 tablespoons sugar, or to taste
14 oz (400 g) can of haricot beans, drained
14 oz (400 g) can of kidney beans, drained
14 oz (400 g) can of chickpeas, drained

TO SERVE (OPTIONAL)
baked potatoes
sour cream

Heat up the oil in a Dutch oven or heavy pot, add the garlic and cook for 2 minutes, then add your cumin and chiles and cook for 1 more minute.

Add your tomato paste, canned tomatoes, stock, cilantro stalks and salt and bring to a boil.

Meanwhile, blanch the runner beans in a separate pot of boiling water for 2 minutes, or until soft and al dente (the time they take will depend on their age), then drain.

Add the lime zest to the tomato sauce, only adding the pieces that you will be able to fish out. Now add the sugar, then tip in your canned beans and chickpeas. Return the stew to a boil. Taste for salt and sugar and adjust if necessary.

Add the lime juice bit by bit, tasting as you go to get the right flavor balance.

When ready to serve, fish out the lime zest pieces, stir in the runner beans and sprinkle with the cilantro leaves. This is perfect served with baked potatoes and sour cream.

Risotto is associated with fine dining and luxury, but that is puzzling to me. You don't need any fancy equipment or expensive ingredients and you can make it from start to finish in 20 minutes. The base of all risottos is just garlic, onion, oil, rice and stock and you get to choose what to flavor it with after that. This is easy, and, if you have any left over, it makes a great arancini ball (see below).

If you haven't used nutritional yeast flakes before, they give a good cheesey flavor to vegan food.

JERUSALEM ARTICHOKE VEGAN RISOTTO

SERVES 2

FOR THE RISOTTO
2 tablespoons olive oil, plus more (optional) to serve
2 shallots, finely chopped
2 garlic cloves, crushed
5½ oz (150 g) Jerusalem artichokes (sunchokes), peeled and grated
1¼ cups (250 g) arborio rice
2 tablespoons white wine vinegar
3½ cups (800 ml) hot vegetable stock
3–4 tablespoons soy cream
4 tablespoons nutritional yeast flakes (see recipe introduction)
2 tablespoons soy sauce
squeeze of lemon juice

TO SERVE
finely chopped parsley leaves
chopped chives
nutmeg

To make the risotto, heat the oil in a pot and fry the shallots and garlic for a few minutes until softened. Add half the grated Jerusalem artichokes and all the rice. Pour in the vinegar and allow the liquid to be absorbed, then reduce the heat to low.

Over this low heat, pour in about 1 cup (240 ml) of the stock and cook, stirring occasionally. Once all the liquid has been absorbed, add half the remaining stock and repeat. Taste the rice and, if it is still too hard, add the remaining stock, though you may not need it all. The risotto will take 15–18 minutes to cook, gently bubbling away, absorbing the stock. Stir as frequently as you feel you can, as that will release the starches from the rice for a creamy texture. And don't worry: whatever you may have heard, risotto will still work even if you're not standing slaving over it and stirring constantly.

To finish, stir in the remaining grated artichoke, then add the soy cream, yeast flakes, soy sauce and lemon juice. Stir well and check that the risotto is not too dry. It may need more liquid, so if you have run out of stock, add a little water.

Sprinkle with a little olive oil, if you like, then scatter with the herbs and grate over some nutmeg to serve.

Tricks of the Trade

Form cooked, chilled risotto into balls, dip each ball in batter (use the batter for Henry's chicken goujons, see page 134, using a vegan Worcestershire sauce alternative), then into a dish of panko crumbs to coat all over. Deep-fry until golden all over and serve with a tomato-based dipping sauce (see page 106), if you like.

This recipe works with all root vegetables: carrot, rutabaga or even celeriac (celery root), all full of fiber, full of goodness. So often we just boil these vegetables—serving them as something on the side to bulk out the meal—but they are wonderful as the star of the show and make a great snack, perfect for party food.

PARSNIP & OREGANO FRITTERS

SERVES 2 FOR LUNCH

FOR THE FRITTERS
1 large parsnip, peeled and grated
1 scallion, sliced
1 teaspoon sea salt
1 tablespoon all-purpose flour
1 tablespoon cornstarch
1 egg, lightly beaten (or see below for a vegan alternative)
leaves from 1 oregano sprig, chopped
1–2 tablespoons olive oil, plus more if needed
1 garlic clove, halved

FOR THE DIP
3 tablespoons mayonnaise (vegan, if needed)
1 tablespoon tomato paste
½ teaspoon chile flakes
leaves from 1 oregano sprig, chopped
pinch of sugar

Mix the parsnip, scallion and salt together in a bowl. Stir in the all-purpose flour and cornstarch, then the egg, and finally the oregano.

Heat the oil in a frying pan over medium heat.

Spoon heaped tablespoons of your parsnip mix into the pan: they should sizzle on arrival! If they don't, wait another minute before you start spooning them in. Cook over the medium heat for 2 minutes until golden, then turn over and cook until golden brown on both sides. Sometimes, if they aren't brown enough, I keep turning them until they're brown, crispy and delicious. Just at the end, put the garlic clove in to flavor them.

Mix all your dip ingredients together in a bowl, stirring in a pinch of salt.

Enjoy the fritters straight away with the dip, or let them cool and take them with you for an on-the-go lunch.

Tricks of the Trade

If you don't have an egg, or want to keep the recipe vegan, replace the egg with a spoon or two of water and replace the mayo in the dip with vegan mayo.

Fish

Growing up, we would often eat fish at least three times a week. Mam fed us fish for nutrition, while Dad fed us fish for the pure delight of it. I have vivid memories of glorious gurnard dinners and of my father, tea towel thrown over his shoulder, big chopping knife in his right hand and sneaky Guinness in his left (perfectly poured). If I'm honest, when my dad cooked, there wasn't a huge variation in the meal he produced, though the type of fish would change. His style was: pat of butter in a frying pan; sliced onions and mushrooms in; a bit of Mam's stock; a red pepper; a few herbs. That would be the sauce. Greek salad on the side. Then the grilled fish, often red or grey gurnard; he'd always get a good deal on gurnard, so he'd be delighted with himself.

Dad would go to the fishmonger and quiz them to bits. He now does this to me and it drives me round the bend, because he listens to none of the answers and just does his own thing... but he really enjoys the discussion, so I can't help getting sucked in each time. His heartfelt appreciation of food and its wonders is something I am grateful to have been raised with, but if I'm truly honest, I'm very lucky that my mother was such a great cook: it was the magical combination of Dad's excitement and Mam's talent that pulled out some wonderful meals.

Some of the recipes in this chapter may sound fancy, but they usually aren't complicated or time-consuming. We often see the humble fish pie as easy—when actually a piece of roasted cod with a white wine sauce is something you could whip up in a fraction of the time—so while my dad's fish pie is pretty great, don't forget to try something new to you, too.

As far back as I can remember, my father Joe took me to street markets, butchers and fishmongers. He loves food and understands it, but often doesn't have my mother's patience when it comes to recipes. If I had a coin for every time my father called me asking me for a recipe—and then did the complete opposite of what I had advised—I'd be a rich woman. I concluded he wasn't writing anything down and just assumed he'd remember it. So, instead of relying on the phone, I started to cook recipes with him when I was home. He would often command my niece Katelyn, or my sister Sarah, to write down what we were doing. So, I started to write the recipes down myself, give them to him, then show him how to make them, too. This resulted in my father really getting stuck in.

Here is a recipe my father managed to follow once, before he lost the scrap of paper. Now, he asks me for it every six weeks (and then loses the paper again). It has parsnips, cabbage and caraway, but trust me, it is delicious. I use smoked fish for a more complex flavor which, in the right amount, does not overpower the pie. Plus because Joe Haugh flippin' loves smoked fish.

DAD'S FISH PIE FROM HOWTH

SERVES 4

FOR THE TOPPING
2 lb 3 oz (1 kg) all-purpose potatoes
1 teaspoon sea salt
3½ tablespoons salted butter, plus more if needed
scant ½ cup (100 ml) warm milk, or as needed
1 egg yolk

FOR THE FILLING
14 oz (400 g) mussels
3½ tablespoons salted butter
1 garlic clove, finely sliced
1 teaspoon caraway seeds
1 onion, chopped
¼ white cabbage, chopped
2 parsnips, peeled and grated
scant 1 cup (200 ml) white wine
3½ tablespoons water
scant ½ cup (100 ml) heavy cream
1 cup (250 ml) milk
2 tablespoons all-purpose flour
7 oz (200 g) skinless natural smoked haddock, cut into ¾ in (2 cm) cubes
3½ oz (100 g) skinless salmon fillet (Mam's favorite!), chopped into 6 pieces
sea salt and cracked black pepper

The first job is to get that buttery mash on the go. Peel your potatoes, cut them in half and put them in a pot of cold water with the salt. Set over high heat and bring to a boil, then reduce the heat to a simmer and cook until you can slip a small knife into a potato with ease. (If you try to cook your potatoes in already-hot water, they are likely to overcook on the outside but be hard on the inside. As with most root veg, they are best started in cold water.)

Push the hot potatoes through a potato ricer, or use a masher (see overleaf) into a large bowl. Add the butter and warm milk until the mash is soft enough to make little peaks. Taste your mash: you're tasting for salt and butter and the decision is in your hands whether to add more. Stir in the egg yolk.

If any mussels are open, tap them to see if they close. You are checking to see if they are alive, as they will only close if they are. Discard the shells that stay open. To prepare the mussels, pull off the "beards," which are the hairy strands emerging from the shells and are actually bits of the rope the mussels were grown on. If any mussels are cracked, discard them. Rinse briefly to remove any debris from the shells.

For the filling, melt the butter in a large pot over medium heat and add your garlic and caraway. Stir for a minute, then add your onion and a pinch of salt. Cook over low heat until the

onion can be squashed between your finger and thumb. Next add your chopped cabbage and grated parsnips, pour in the wine and cook for a further 5 minutes.

Add your mussels with the measured water and, with the lid off, cook on a simmer. You have the chance to delight in watching your mussels pop open while cooking! Scoop them out as they pop open, to avoid them overcooking, stirring from time to time so all the shells have a chance to get close to the heat. Let the mussel stock absorb into your vegetables, creating some real magic. When you have spooned your mussels out of the pot and they are cool enough to handle, remove the meat from the shells. (If any mussels refuse to open after 5–8 minutes, discard them.) Pass the mussel juices through a sieve into the pan with the vegetables, then stir in the cream and milk.

Mix your flour in a small bowl with a little water to make a smooth paste, then stir this into the vegetables once the mixture is bubbling. Once the flour is cooked (a matter of 1–2 minutes), pour the sauce into a baking dish, which should measure 10–11 in (25–28 cm) in diameter, or the equivalent.

Place your chopped fish on top with your mussels evenly, then layer your mash on that. Your pie is now ready to go in the oven, or to be covered and popped in the fridge for a later time.

Preheat the oven to 425°F (220°C).

Cook the pie in the oven for 30 minutes if you're doing it straight away, or for 45 minutes if it is from the fridge. What you're looking for is fish pie that is golden brown and measures 150°F (65°C) in the center on a kitchen thermometer, or use the metal skewer test (see opposite).

When your pie comes out of the oven, generously crack black pepper over the top.

I love to serve fish pie with a crunchy salad, or with peas.

Tricks of the Trade

Once your potatoes are cooked, it's best to finish the mash straight away. This is because the potato starch is at its prime and is ready to absorb the maximum amount of milk and butter. Push the potatoes through a potato ricer, or use a masher. Add the butter and warmed milk. If you make mash with cold potatoes, their starch is "set" and isn't ready to absorb liquids, so, when you stir, the starch begins to become gluey.

The skewer test: fish

Take your fish out of the oven, steamer or frying pan and put a skewer into the top middle of the protein, touching the base of the tray or plate it is resting on. Leave for 10 seconds, making sure you hold your thumb on the skewer at the top of where the protein is, then remove the skewer and place it on the inside of your wrist. This is something you must get a feel for and isn't as tricky as you think, once you do it a few times. I recommend checking the temperature of your fish every 2 minutes and feel the temperature rise on your wrist, resulting in you instinctively teaching yourself.

Delicate white fish and salmon =
warm-hot =
125°F (50°C)

Meaty monkfish =
slightly hotter =
140°F (58°C)

It is easier to cook fish when you have a kitchen thermometer, since fish is ready at a lower temperature than meat. White fish is cooked when the flesh flakes. White fish such as cod, halibut and haddock as well as salmon should produce a skewer that feels warm-hot (and/or measures 125°F/50°C). Monkfish is a meaty fish and tends to need a slightly higher temperature, so the skewer should feel slightly hotter 140°F (58°C). I still recommend resting all fish, as residual heat (see page 201) will keep it cooking as it sits.

I love fish cakes. We grew up eating a lot of fish, since my father loves going to the fishmonger for a good chat, while buying kilos of fish. He has checked behind my mother's ears to see if she has sprouted gills, since she eats so much salmon... Fish cakes can be made from leftovers, but also can celebrate your favorite fish. It is so easy to add different spices and flavors to them, and here I use mustard, a handy ingredient that's not just for sandwiches!

There are hundreds of fish cake recipes online, but they can lack seasoning and interest. I've kept this recipe simple, but with an explosion of flavor. By marinating your fish first, you get flavor to its core, while by flavoring the mash with smoked mackerel you create layered deliciousness in every bite. What fish you use is up to you; I've chosen salmon, but haddock or basa work, too.

MARINATED FISH CAKES

Mix together all the ingredients for the marinade in a bowl and gently stir in the salmon chunks. Marinate for at least 10 and up to 30 minutes.

Now make the fish cakes. Add the mashed potatoes to the salmon and marinade, along with the smoked mackerel and a pinch of salt, and mix well with your hands. If the mash was a little wet, you may need to add more panko crumbs to help the mixture come together.

Dust a work surface and your hands with flour and shape the mixture into 4 good-sized fish cakes, flattening them into discs. Dip the fish cakes into more flour to coat all over.

In a flat dish, mix the scant ½ cup (50 g) flour with a pinch of salt, then pour in enough water, stirring, to form a batter about as thick as heavy cream. (If you stick your finger in, the batter should coat it.)

Put the panko crumbs in another flat dish.

FOR THE FISH AND MARINADE

½ garlic clove, crushed
2 tablespoons olive oil
1 teaspoon Dijon mustard
1 teaspoon sea salt
1 tablespoon Lilliput or Nonpareil (small) capers, plus more (optional) to serve
1 tablespoon chopped dill
7 oz (200 g) skinless salmon fillet, chopped

FOR THE FISH CAKES

7 oz (200 g) mashed potatoes
1 smoked mackerel fillet, skinned and chopped
3 cups (150 g) panko crumbs, plus more if needed
scant ½ cup (50 g) all-purpose flour, plus more to dust and coat
2 tablespoons vegetable oil
lemon wedges, plus finely grated lemon zest (optional), to serve
sea salt

FOR THE HERBY MAYO

3 tablespoons mayonnaise, or thick Greek-style yogurt
1 teaspoon Dijon mustard
1 tablespoon chopped tarragon leaves, plus more (optional) to serve
2 tablespoons chopped dill leaves, plus more (optional) to serve
2 tablespoons chopped parsley leaves, plus more (optional) to serve

Dip the floured fish cakes in the batter to coat all over, then into the panko crumbs, again until entirely covered.

Heat the oil in a frying pan over medium heat. Add the fish cakes and cook for 5 minutes, until they start to turn golden brown on the bottom. Use a fish slice or large spatula to gently turn them over and continue to cook for 3–5 minutes until golden brown.

Meanwhile, mix all the ingredients for the herby mayo in a bowl.

Spread a teaspoon of the herby mayo on top of each fish cake; this not only adds flavor but helps to hold the herbs, capers and lemon zest in place, if you're feeling that way inclined.

On each plate, dollop a heaped spoon of herby mayo. Put a fish cake half on the herby mayo, then scatter over herbs, capers and lemon zest, if you like. Serve with lemon wedges. These are lovely with a salad.

Tricks of the Trade

If you think you won't need all four fish cakes at the same time, they freeze well. Cook them from frozen, with a drizzle of oil on top, in an oven preheated to 410°F (210°C) for 30 minutes, turning them over halfway through.

There are many ingredients which are unfairly dismissed, and, in my opinion, oats are one of those. There is a lot more you can use them for than just oatmeal. Since they usually come priced very affordably and in a big bag, I have a few recipes for quick and easy ways to use them up (see pages 206 and 220). And eating oats regularly can help to reduce your cholesterol.

Ireland and Scotland are two countries whose climate isn't great for growing wheat, but is suitable for oats. As a kid, when my mother pressed oats onto the skin of mackerel, I just thought it was another of her money-saving hacks, but actually it's something many of our Celtic ancestors would have done.

OAT-CRUSTED HAKE WITH SMOKED MACKEREL SAUCE

SERVES 2

1 cup (40 g) jumbo oats, or use thick rolled oats if you can't find jumbo
4 teaspoons vegetable oil, plus more for the oats
¼ cup (40 g) sesame seeds
2 tablespoons coriander seeds
2 × 5½ oz (150 g) skin-on hake pieces
1 egg white
3 oz (80 g) spinach
3 tablespoons House vinaigrette, or Airing-cupboard vinaigrette (see pages 28 and 181)
sea salt

FOR THE SAUCE
1 garlic clove, crushed
thyme sprig
2 tablespoons salted butter, plus a pat for the spinach
½ onion, chopped
3½ tablespoons white wine
⅔ cup (150 ml) milk
3½ tablespoons heavy cream
2 fillets of smoked mackerel, skinned
freshly ground black pepper

Preheat the oven to 400°F (200°C).

Rub the oats in oil and a pinch of salt, put them on a baking sheet and pat into an even layer. Bake for 8 minutes. At the same time, place the sesame seeds and coriander seeds on 2 separate small baking sheets and bake in the oven for 5 minutes for sesame, and 3 minutes for coriander. Mix together the oats and toasted seeds, then tip onto a sheet of paper towels and allow to cool.

Now start the sauce. Sweat the garlic and thyme in the butter with a pinch of salt for 2 minutes over medium-low heat. Add the onion and cook for 5–10 minutes or until the onion is very soft, then add the white wine and reduce until it has boiled away. Add the milk and cream and bring to a boil, remove the thyme, then add the mackerel and purée in a blender until silky-smooth (see page 37). Season well with pepper.

Season the hake pieces with salt, brush the skin side with egg white and pat the oat mixture generously on top to form a crust. Bake for 6–10 minutes, depending on thickness, then use the metal skewer test to check it is cooked (see page 113).

Meanwhile, return your sauce to a boil and wilt your spinach in a separate pan with a pat of butter and a pinch of salt. Shake your vinaigrette to re-emulsify, then spoon onto the oat crust once the hake is fully cooked and ready to serve.

Pour the sauce into warmed bowls and rest the fish on top, nestling the wilted spinach on the side.

Who doesn't love a nice piece of crispy fried fish? I have a great tip for you to help you create a crispy coating: cornstarch. If you are nervous of frying fish, cornstarch will help you out. It removes excess moisture from the skin that can otherwise make fish stick to your frying pan. Or, to play it even safer, just season the cod with salt and bake it in an oven preheated to 400°F (200°C) for 8-10 minutes.

ROASTED COD WITH WHITE WINE & MUSSEL SAUCE

Start with the sauce. If any mussels are open, tap them to see if they close. You are checking to see if they are alive, as they will only close if they are. Discard the shells that stay open.

To prepare the mussels, pull off the "beards," which are the hairy strands emerging from the shell and are actually bits of the rope the mussels were grown on. With a small knife, scrape off any barnacles. If any mussels are cracked, discard them. Rinse briefly to remove any debris from the shells.

Melt your butter in a pot over low heat. Add the garlic, onion and thyme and cook for 5 minutes. You want to make sure the onion is fully cooked before moving to the next stage: you should be able to squash the pieces between your finger and thumb.

Add your white wine and boil until it's almost completely gone. Pour in the stock and bring to a boil. Now add your mussels. I like to watch them pop open, so use a wooden spoon to stir and spoon them out as they open, to avoid overcooking. This should take around 5 minutes. Discard any shells that do not open after 5–8 minutes.

Pour the entire contents of the pot through a sieve and shake out all the juices. Return it to the pot and add the cream, then bring to a boil and taste, adjusting the seasoning if needed (see below right). Store your mussels in a baking dish to put back into the oven to warm through before serving.

FOR THE SAUCE

7 oz (200 g) mussels
1 tablespoon unsalted butter
1 garlic clove, crushed
1 small onion, finely chopped
  or grated
1 thyme sprig
⅓ cup (75 ml) dry white wine
⅓ cup (75 ml) fish or vegetable
  stock
scant ½ cup (100 ml) heavy
  cream
sea salt and freshly ground
  black pepper

FOR THE COD

2 × 3½ oz (100 g) portions of cod,
  skin on or off, as you prefer
½ cup (50 g) cornstarch (or see
  recipe introduction)
3 tablespoons vegetable oil
2 tablespoons House vinaigrette,
  or Airing-cupboard vinaigrette
  (see pages 28 and 181)

Sprinkle the pieces of cod on all sides with salt and set aside for 3–4 minutes; I recommend this with any fish, as it will let the flesh soak in the seasoning and firm up, too. Spread the cornstarch on a large plate. Dip the pieces of cod in the cornstarch, either skin side down if it has skin, or on the side where it had skin, if it is skinless.

Preheat the oven to 400°F (200°C).

Heat up a frying pan, big enough for the portions of fish, over medium-high heat. Add the vegetable oil. Place the fish in the pan, cornstarch side down. Wait until you see golden brown color on the side of the fish in contact with the pan, and the fish flesh changing color up the sides of the pieces from translucent to white. When it is white halfway up the sides (about 3 minutes), flip it over and cook for another 2 minutes, then take the pan off the heat for the fish to rest.

While the fish is resting, bring your sauce back to a boil and put your dish of mussels in the oven just to warm through.

Shake up the vinaigrette to re-emulsify, then drizzle it on top of your fish.

Serve the fish, mussels and sauce with shredded and blanched cabbage and creamy mash, or even a crisp salad.

Tricks of the Trade

I cannot stress this enough: taste what you are making at *every* stage and adjust its seasoning before you continue to cook. This layering really results in much more flavorful food.

Once monkfish is mentioned, you know you're in for a special meal, because it's a luxurious, meaty fish. If you can't get your hands on monkfish, this recipe will also work extremely well with cod.

MARINATED MONKFISH, BUTTERNUT SQUASH & PUMPKIN SEEDS

SERVES 2

FOR THE FISH AND MARINADE
1–2 tablespoons thick Greek-style yogurt
½ teaspoon smoked paprika
½ teaspoon hot paprika
½ teaspoon honey
½ teaspoon sea salt
squeeze of lime juice (about ¼ lime)
2 × 5½ oz (150 g) monkfish portions, skin and membrane removed by the fishmonger

FOR THE PUMPKIN SEEDS AND RICE
4 tablespoons pumpkin seeds
1 tablespoon vegetable oil
⅓ cup (75 g) brown rice
1½ tablespoons salted butter
sea salt

FOR THE SQUASH
1 butternut squash, deseeded and trimmed
3½ tablespoons salted butter
½ teaspoon sea salt
leaves from a bunch of basil, larger leaves ripped

Preheat the oven to 400°F (200°C).

Mix the yogurt, smoked paprika, hot paprika, honey, salt and lime juice in a bowl, add your monkfish, turn to coat and place in the fridge until you are ready to cook.

Mix the pumpkin seeds and oil on a small baking sheet with a sprinkle of salt. Cook in the oven for 4 minutes.

Bring the brown rice to a boil in a saucepan of salted water and simmer for 18 minutes, or according to the package instructions. Drain, then add the butter and season to taste with salt. This can be served at room temperature, or warmed up in the oven or microwave, before serving.

Peel and chop the butternut squash. Place on a baking sheet and cook for 30 minutes, or until you can squash it with a fork. Crush the butternut squash with a fork or a masher, adding your butter, ½ teaspoon of salt and the larger ripped basil leaves at the end.

Line a baking sheet with parchment paper and lay your marinated monkfish on top. Bake in the oven for 7 minutes.

Spoon your butternut squash onto plates, make a well in the center and fill with the brown rice.

Place your monkfish on top and scatter with the toasted pumpkin seeds and the smaller basil leaves. A very elegant presentation with minimum effort.

Tricks of the Trade

You could also grill the monkfish for 3–4 minutes on each side, if you prefer: I actually quite like it when the top of the marinade has been slightly charred by the heat of the grill.

This dish was inspired by my time living in Paris, working for Gualtiero Marchesi at Hotel Lotti. I was the pastry chef and would come in on my days off to learn anything I could from the other sections in the kitchen. It was here that I first tasted vitello tonnato—*poached veal with a tuna, caper and anchovy sauce— which remains to this day my desert island dish. In this recipe, I remove the tuna from the sauce and serve the anchovy-caper dressing with a rare tuna steak instead of the meat. It can be eaten hot or cold, but I prefer it cold. The quality of the anchovies is key here, and you need both fresh silver-colored marinated anchovies and those canned in oil.*

You'll have more dressing than you need, but my god you'll use it. I could eat it like a yogurt. It's also wonderful on crusty bread.

HERB CRUSTED TUNA LOIN
WITH CAPER & ANCHOVY DRESSING

SERVES 2

FOR THE DRESSING
3½ oz (100 g) fresh marinated
  anchovies
3½ oz (100 g) salted anchovies in
  oil, ideally Ortiz brand
2½ tablespoons capers
finely grated zest of 1 lemon
¼ garlic clove, grated
scant ½ cup (100 ml) vegetable
  oil, plus a little more for
  the tuna
3½ tablespoons extra virgin
  olive oil

FOR THE TUNA
2 tuna loin steaks
4 teaspoons Dijon mustard
leaves from a bunch of flat-leaf
  parsley, chopped
leaves from ½ bunch of tarragon,
  chopped
sea salt and freshly ground
  black pepper

TO SERVE
bunch of round radishes, sliced,
  left whole, or both
1 fennel bulb, shaved on a
  mandoline or grated on a grater

For the dressing, place both types of anchovies, the capers, lemon zest and garlic in a food processor and pulse-blend, while slowly adding both types of oil, until you have an emulsified sauce.

Heat a griddle pan over very high heat.

Season the tuna steaks, rub them with oil and sear in the very hot pan on all sides, for only 3 seconds on each side. Transfer to a plate. Rub the tuna with the mustard and cover with most of the chopped herbs and some salt and pepper.

Mix the radishes and fennel with the remaining herbs.

Halve the tuna steaks so you can see the lovely pink centers, then serve them on the sauce with the radishes and fennel, which you can treat as a salad (or use for dipping, if you have left any radishes whole. Thank me later).

Now this was a special of Henry, my stepson, which has the same batter-and-panko coating as the chicken version (see page 134). I recommend making more than you need and freezing these; that way, when you don't feel like cooking, you can just grab them from the freezer and grill or fry them for five minutes on each side.

FISH GOUJONS WITH MUSHY GARDEN PEAS & SPICY SWEET POTATO FRIES

SERVES 2–3

FOR THE FISH
2 × 5½ oz (150 g) portions of skinless cod fillet
5 tablespoons all-purpose flour, plus more to dust
4 tablespoons Worcestershire sauce
scant ½ cup (100 ml) water
4 cups (200 g) panko crumbs
sea salt

FOR THE CHIPS
3 sweet potatoes (about 7 oz/200 g each)
3 tablespoons sunflower oil, plus more for the fish
½ teaspoon chile flakes
1 teaspoon cumin seeds

FOR THE PEAS
3½ tablespoons salted butter
1 garlic clove, halved
2⅓ cups (300 g) frozen peas

TO SERVE (OPTIONAL)
handful of mint leaves, ripped
lemon wedges

Preheat the oven to 410°F (210°C).

Cut the cod into ¼–½ in (0.5–1 cm) thick strips, as long or as short as you like, then season on both sides with salt. Dust the strips with flour.

In a shallow dish, whisk together the Worcestershire sauce, measured water and the 5 tablespoons of flour until you have a smooth batter. Tip the panko crumbs into another shallow dish.

Dip your floured cod pieces in the Worcestershire sauce batter, let it drip a little, then dip into the crumbs. Make sure your fish pieces are completely covered in crumbs.

Lay the cod on a baking sheet to cook later.

Peel your sweet potatoes and cut into ½ in (1 cm) thick fries, then place in a bowl and sprinkle with the oil, spices and 3 pinches of salt. Mix, then place on a baking sheet lined with parchment paper.

Cook the fries for 20–30 minutes: you want them brown on the outside and soft on the inside.

After the fries have been cooking for about 15 minutes, drizzle a little oil over your fish goujons before placing them in the oven. Cook for 10–15 minutes or until golden brown on each side.

Meanwhile, make the peas. Put the butter and garlic in a small pan. When the garlic is about to turn brown, add the peas and a pinch of salt, give it a stir, then tip into a food processor and pulse-blend until the peas are crushed. You don't want a purée here, so watch the blending process carefully (see page 37).

Serve a generous dollop of mushy peas on the plates, place the fish goujons on top and serve the fries on the side.

You can elevate the flavor with some ripped mint leaves and a lemon wedge, if you like.

Meat

What's the most popular meat eaten in your home? I could take a guess at chicken breast, or maybe ground beef. Growing up, we didn't eat a lot of chicken breast, but my god we had a fair few "mince dinners." Of course, I've a few chicken breast and ground beef recipes in here, but we have lots of other wonderful ingredients to choose from that don't have to break the bank and can really liven up the food you cook. For instance, when I think of the bad rep black pudding gets, it breaks my heart. We are all trying to be more mindful of the environment and sustainability and avoid waste, yet one ingredient that is wasted in abundance is blood. There is nutritional benefit to black pudding and it can transform a simple pasta dish or casserole, to give far more flavor.

I cook a lot at home, in fact almost every single day, for us and our two-year-old son, Oisín. My main focus is introducing the little guy to foods I know are good for him and that he might find tasty... but, of course, I also get to enjoy them with him. We rarely eat takeout, not out of food purism but because I've always got so much food in the house that I feel guilty not using it up.

Sometimes I like to spend hours in the kitchen, chopping, stirring, nurturing something delicious onto the plates, whereas on other evenings I want to throw something tasty together quickly without any effort. The meat recipes in this chapter are a mixture of both: all for different moods and different days, but each one deeply satisfying and very doable.

Henry is my stepson and this is the first thing I cooked for him when he was only a little boy. When I first met him, he already loved chicken goujons, so I started to work on a recipe that we could make together. I didn't realize it would be the first recipe I would create for my own family, but now I know that I'll be making it for the rest of my life. Perhaps for grandkids one day. So it means a lot to me.

Henry and I have a secret ingredient that we found made a big difference: Worcestershire sauce. Henry is all grown up now, but every time he comes to stay, I have a batch of his goujons ready.

When our son Oisín was born, Henry brought him a little baby lion stuffed animal—Lenny—and that's who you can see in this photo.

HENRY'S CHICKEN GOUJONS

SERVES 4

2 boneless, skinless chicken
  breasts
5 tablespoons all-purpose flour,
  plus more to dust
¼ cup (60 ml) Worcestershire
  sauce
scant ½ cup (100 ml) water
3 cups (150 g) panko crumbs
vegetable oil
sea salt

FOR THE DIPPING SAUCE
6 tablespoons mayonnaise
1 tablespoon Worcestershire
  sauce

Cut the chicken breasts into ½ in (1 cm) thick strips, as long or as short as you like, then season them on both sides with salt. Dust the strips with flour.

In a shallow dish, whisk together the Worcestershire sauce, measured water and the 5 tablespoons of flour until you have a smooth batter. Tip the panko crumbs into another shallow dish.

Dip your floured chicken pieces in the Worcestershire sauce batter, let it drip a little, then dip the chicken into your crumbs. Make sure the pieces are completely covered in crumbs.

Heat up a frying pan with just enough oil to cover the base. Place in the goujons and cook until golden brown all over, which should take about 3 minutes on each side.

(You can also bake these if you prefer, in an oven preheated to 410°F/210°C. Lay the chicken on a roasting pan and drizzle a little oil on top. Cook until golden brown, about 10 minutes.)

Meanwhile, mix the mayo with the Worcestershire sauce in a small bowl.

Serve the chicken goujons with your Worcestershire mayonnaise. Some crispy potato wedges on the side are always good here.

I've always been interested in every type of food and eat anything put in front of me, including blood clams (I must admit I wouldn't recommend those). But I have only started to cook Asian dishes at home in the last five or ten years. This recipe is off-the-charts delicious, quick and easy. I love if I have any left over, because I think it's flippin' delicious eaten cold from the fridge when I get home after a long day and night at the restaurant.

This dish can be adjusted to include whatever vegetables you have in your kitchen. I chose to base the version here on carrots and kale, because that's what I always—and I mean always—have in mine. But cauliflower or broccoli would work very well instead of carrots, or any cabbage instead of kale. The seeds give great texture but also good nutrition to the meal, especially if you wanted to go meatless. The texture from the seeds and the aroma from the sesame oil at the end make such an impact.

TUESDAY NIGHT QUICK STIR-FRY

SERVES 2

5½ oz (150 g) minute steak
½ teaspoon baking soda
3 tablespoons vegetable oil
2 garlic cloves, finely sliced
1 thumb-sized piece of root
   ginger, finely sliced
pinch of chile flakes
2 scallions, white and green parts
   separated and finely sliced
2 carrots, cut into strips, or into
   ribbons with a vegetable peeler
1 tablespoon honey
2 tablespoons soy sauce
½ teaspoon black sesame seeds,
   or white sesame seeds if you
   can't find black
big handful of kale, coarse ribs
   removed, leaves shredded
1 tablespoon toasted sesame oil
1 tablespoon white sesame seeds

Take your minute steak and sprinkle it with the baking soda evenly on each side. Set aside for up to 10 minutes. This will make it super-tender and melty. Rinse the steak briefly to remove the baking soda and slice it finely.

Pour the oil into a saucepan or wok, then add the garlic and ginger and cook, stirring, until the garlic is almost turning brown. Throw in the chile flakes and scallion whites, then add the sliced beef and stir.

Now tip in the carrots and stir for 1 minute.

Add the honey, soy sauce, black sesame seeds and kale. Stir and cook for 2 minutes, just to start cooking the kale down.

Finish with the sesame oil, white sesame seeds and scallion greens, then serve.

One of the main reasons I decided to write this book is that I didn't realize until recently that so many people still cooked recipes I had given them years ago. Now, this recipe I have shared with more people than you could shake a stick at. I have taught it to best friends, sisters and brothers; they all have added their spin and make it time and again. It's a really wonderful dish. Now it's yours.

A long time ago I did a stage (that's a period of time you work for free in a professional kitchen) at the Cinnamon Club in London. I was in awe of the flavors and ingredients I saw there. Indian cooking is very different to the Modern European style of food I'd been trained in, but there are many processes that cross over. I feel that learning even just a little bit about Indian food and cooking styles has made me understand flavor more. I memorized a handful of recipes and I wrote every single thing I saw down in my notebook. At the Cinnamon Club, they had a tomato-based recipe called "old Delhi" curry. This version has slightly altered over time, but the core values I learned from chef Vivek Singh still ring true.

The wonderful thing about homemade curries—apart from the fact that they are delicious and also a great way to use up what you have in your fridge—is that the list of ingredients is merely a guide. The marinating of the chicken here is optional, so skip it if you do not have the time, but you do get the benefit of an extra layer of flavor.

This freezes so well that making a bigger batch is a great idea, to keep for a day when you don't feel like cooking.

ANNA'S WEDNESDAY NIGHT CURRY

Mix the chicken and all the marinade ingredients well together in a bowl with a pinch of sea salt, then cover and leave to marinate for 10–20 minutes.

Put the oil in a large Dutch oven or heavy pot over medium heat. Add your garlic and ginger and cook for 2 minutes, then stir in the spices until they are aromatic. Then tip in your chopped onions. Cook until the onions are sweet. Don't skip this step: the onions being cooked until their sugars are properly released make a huge difference to the final curry.

When the onions are ready, add your tomatoes and tomato paste and cook for 20 minutes.

**FOR THE CHICKEN
AND MARINADE**

9 oz (250 g) skinless boneless
  chicken thighs or breasts,
  cut into bite-sized cubes
½ garlic clove, crushed
1 teaspoon finely grated
  root ginger
1 teaspoon sweet paprika
½ teaspoon hot paprika,
  or to taste
3 tablespoons thick Greek-
  style yogurt, plus more
  (optional) to serve
juice of ¼ lemon
sea salt

FOR THE CURRY

3 tablespoons vegetable oil
3 garlic cloves, crushed
2 in (5 cm) thumb of root ginger,
  finely grated
2 green cardamom pods, crushed
1 tablespoon cumin seeds
1 teaspoon hot chile powder, or
  to taste
1 tablespoon sweet paprika
2 onions, finely chopped
14 oz (400 g) can of chopped
  tomatoes, or 8 fresh tomatoes,
  chopped
2 tablespoons tomato paste
1 red pepper, cut into bite-
  sized cubes
3½ oz (100 g) butternut squash,
  cut into bite-sized cubes
14 oz (400 g) can of coconut milk
1–2 tablespoons sugar, to taste
juice of 1–2 limes, to taste
cilantro leaves, to serve

Now add your red pepper and butternut squash and cook for 10 minutes, or until the squash pieces are tender.

Finally, add your chicken and its marinade and cook for 10 minutes.

Pour in the coconut milk and taste: this is where you can create magic. When you taste your curry, ask yourself: is it hot enough? If not, add some extra chile powder gradually. (If it's too spicy, see below.) And salt! Don't forget to taste in case you need a little extra salt. And as for sweetness and acidity balance, use your judgement about how much sugar and lime juice to add, to round out the flavors.

Rip over the cilantro leaves and ripple with more yogurt, if you like, both for a bit of visual drama and for that cool contrast to the spicy curry.

Serve with plain boiled rice and/or naan or other flatbread (see page 52 for homemade), as your curry will be bursting with flavor and the contrast of the plain rice or naan will complement and balance the heat, so each bite is even more delicious.

Tricks of the Trade

Curry too spicy? Well, just add some sugar and maybe a dash of cream, or coconut cream, if you have it, then taste and adjust again until you're happy with the flavor.

I created this recipe for the first ever photo shoot we did for my restaurant, Myrtle, back in 2019. I was very delighted with the dish, and excited to be shooting. The place where I was living at the time had a floor which made an excellent backdrop for photography, so we were shooting this plate of chicken on the floor.

I put the plate down and, just as I turned around, my little dog—who was only a puppy at the time—scooped a crispy thigh into her mouth and bolted through the back door. She left me standing in the kitchen, staring at the chicken hanging out of her mouth and watching her chow down.

I can't blame her. Who doesn't love a crispy thigh?

CRISPY CHICKEN THIGHS WITH SPINACH PURÉE, GOAT CHEESE & QUICK PICKLED RED ONION

SERVES 2

2 tablespoons vegetable oil
4 skin-on boneless chicken thighs
½ garlic clove, very finely sliced
2 tablespoons salted butter
7 oz (200 g) spinach, plus more small spinach leaves to serve
pinch of sugar
3 oz (80 g) goat cheese
sea salt and freshly ground black pepper

FOR THE QUICK PICKLED ONION
3½ tablespoons water
scant ½ cup (100 ml) white wine vinegar
¼ cup (50 g) sugar
1 red onion, finely sliced

Set a frying pan over medium heat and pour in the oil.

Season the chicken thighs with salt and pepper, place in the pan skin side down and cook until the skin becomes crispy; this will take around 10 minutes.

For the quick pickled onion, pour the measured water and vinegar into a saucepan with the sugar and a pinch of salt, then place over high heat and bring to a boil. Place the finely sliced onion in a heatproof bowl, then pour over the brine. It will be ready to eat in 5 minutes. (If your onion is more thickly sliced, boil it along with the brine for a second or 2 first.)

Meanwhile, put the garlic in a medium pot with the butter and a pinch of salt and cook for 2 minutes. Add your spinach and sugar and stir while the spinach wilts down. Put it into a blender and process to a purée (see page 181).

Your chicken should almost be done. Check it's crispy and, if it is, flip the thighs onto their other sides while you get your plates and silverware ready. After a minute or two, you're ready to serve.

Serve the spinach purée on plates or in bowls and add the goat cheese, broken into chunks. Place your chicken thighs on top and serve with the quick pickled onions and a scattering of extra spinach leaves.

The name here might sound fancy, but my goodness is it a simple dish. There are layers upon layers of flavor, but it's easily put together while relaxing to a favorite podcast.

This needs only plain boiled baby potatoes added to make it into more of a meal, as the sauce is so delicious with the acidity of the tomatoes. There is already loads of flavor going on, so it's nice to have an element on the plate that isn't fighting for attention! If you don't want to use semi-dried tomatoes, Kalamata olives are a great alternative.

CHICKEN FRICASSEE WITH PESTO & SEMI-DRIED TOMATOES

FOR THE PESTO
1 tablespoon pine nuts
bunch of basil
1 garlic clove, crushed or
    finely grated
1 lemon
2½ tablespoons extra virgin
    olive oil
4 teaspoons vegetable oil
scant ½ cup (40 g) finely grated
    Parmesan cheese, or vintage
    Cheddar
sea salt

FOR THE CHICKEN
2 tablespoons vegetable oil
10½ oz (300 g) skin-on boneless
    chicken thighs
1 garlic clove, finely sliced
1 shallot, finely sliced
scant ½ cup (100 ml) white wine
scant ½ cup (100 ml) chicken
    stock
2¾ tablespoons salted butter
1¾ oz (50 g) semi-dried tomatoes
    (the bright red ones)

Put the pine nuts, basil and garlic in a food processor. Zest in the lemon and pulse-blend to keep some texture (see page 37), adding both types of oil slowly along with a pinch of salt, then finally stir in the Parmesan or Cheddar. Taste and add a squeeze of lemon juice.

For the chicken, heat a sauté pan over medium-high heat and add the oil and a sprinkle of salt. Add the chicken, skin side down, and cook until caramelized. Add the garlic and shallot and stir until softened, then pour in the wine and boil until it has nearly disappeared. Pour in the stock and bring to a boil, then stir in the butter and semi-dried tomatoes. Taste to see if it needs more salt.

Serve the fricassee with the pesto.

Listen: in cookbooks, you'll often read about how this or that recipe is a favorite of the author, but this dish is genuinely something that I cook at least three times a month. I love it because it's healthy, satisfying, looks gorgeous and is fun to eat. My fella always has this with flour tortillas; I sometimes do too, but there are always Baby Gem leaves on the table. I prefer them to the tortillas as wrappers.

If you are eating less meat, the same recipe works well with eggplant cut into fingers and treated in the same way as the chicken here.

CHICKEN & BABY GEM TACO NIGHT

I follow a traditional way of making a Mexican salsa. There is a little bit of magic that happens when you take the chopped onion and add the lime juice, put it in a bowl, then stir in the chile, salt and garlic. The salt must go in after the chile; I don't understand why, but that's where the magic seems to come from! Really try to leave this for 5 minutes, if you can, before adding the tomatoes and then the chopped cilantro. It may seem trivial, but it makes a huge difference, just try it and see. The juices that come out from this salsa are so delicious, I want to drink them down on their own with a shot of tequila! Cover the salsa and set aside until you're ready to eat.

Peel the avocado, discard the pit and mash the flesh roughly in a bowl, then add all the other guacamole ingredients with a pinch of salt. You want to keep some texture here, so don't be too thorough about mashing and mixing it.

Chop the chicken into strips about ½ in (1 cm) in width and place them in a bowl. Separately mix the ground spices, chile, salt and sugar briefly, until evenly combined, then stir these through the chicken. Set aside to marinate for 10 minutes.

FOR THE SALSA ROJA

¼ onion, finely chopped
juice of 1 lime
1 jalapeño or other chile,
 finely chopped
1 garlic clove, finely chopped
3 tomatoes, chopped
¼ bunch of cilantro,
 finely chopped
sea salt

FOR THE GUACAMOLE

1 avocado
½ chile, finely chopped
juice of ½ lime
½ shallot, finely chopped

FOR THE CHICKEN

4 large skinless boneless
 chicken thighs
1 teaspoon ground cumin
¼ teaspoon hot paprika
1 red chile, finely sliced
½ teaspoon sea salt
½ teaspoon sugar
3 tablespoons vegetable oil
1 garlic clove, halved
1 red onion, finely sliced
1 red pepper, cut into strips
1 green pepper, cut into strips

TO SERVE

1 cup (100 g) grated Cheddar
 cheese
tortilla chips
6 tablespoons sour cream,
 crème fraîche or thick
 Greek-style yogurt
2 heads of Baby Gem lettuce,
 leaves carefully separated
 and washed

Pour the oil into a pan and cook the chicken until golden brown on one side, then add the garlic and then the onion, cooking for a few minutes before following with both the peppers. You just want to get a nice golden color on your vegetables and for the onion to be sweet, to balance out the spice of the dish, though a little bit of a bite remaining in all the veg is also very welcome.

Meanwhile, get your table ready. A big part of taco night for me is how great the table looks: colorful, appetizing and welcoming. And plenty of it all. I like to put everything down the center, to make it super-easy for every diner to serve themselves. So get your grated cheese in a bowl, tortilla chips in a serving dish, and your salsa, guacamole and sour cream, crème fraîche or yogurt in their own separate little bowls. Have the Baby Gem leaves on a plate and count on everyone needing 4–5 of those as wrappers.

When the chicken mixture is cooked, take it to the table hot and sizzling and build the tacos in the lettuce leaves.

I want to take you back in time to 1999. This was the year that—having seen that I was becoming a keen apprentice cook—my mother bought me my first ever cookbook: The Naked Chef. As far back as I can remember, it was my favorite gift I ever got; it really had an effect on me. I had never before combined ingredients in the way that Jamie Oliver suggested and I cooked so many recipes from that book. The first I tried was his marinated pork chops, so this recipe is inspired by that. The dish also works with pork medallions.

ROSEMARY PORK CHOPS WITH RED ONION & BALSAMIC MARMALADE

SERVES 4

4 thick-cut pork chops on the bone (or see recipe introduction)
1 tablespoon extra virgin olive oil
1½ teaspoons finely chopped rosemary leaves, plus 2–3 longer rosemary sprigs
1 garlic clove, finely chopped
sea salt and freshly ground black pepper

FOR THE POTATO SALAD
1 lb 12 oz (800 g) baby potatoes, halved
3 tablespoons mayonnaise
finely grated zest and juice of 1 lemon
chopped chives

FOR THE MARMALADE
2 tablespoons extra virgin olive oil
1 medium red onion, sliced
2 teaspoons balsamic vinegar
1 tablespoon soft light brown sugar

Preheat the oven to 425°F (220°C). Put the chops in a bowl with the oil, 1 teaspoon of the rosemary, the garlic, salt and pepper and toss well. Leave to marinate for 10 minutes: you'll be surprised how this time can transform your chop from nice to remarkable.

Make the potato salad. Steam the potatoes until a knife slides right through, then leave to cool. Mix in the mayonnaise, lemon zest and juice and the chives and season to taste.

I like to cook a chop on a griddle pan for a good smoky flavor, but you can use a frying pan. Place your chosen pan over low heat and add the chops fat side down (see below). Increase the heat to high and sear the chops, turning, to get great color on each side. Place the long rosemary sprigs in a roasting pan and put the pork on top. Roast for 6–10 minutes, depending on thickness, until cooked through. Leave to rest for 5 minutes.

Meanwhile, make the balsamic marmalade. Heat the olive oil in a medium sauté pan. Fry the onion over low heat for 5–6 minutes, or until well softened, stirring occasionally. Add the vinegar and sugar and bring to a simmer. Cook for a further 2 minutes, stirring.

Spoon the potato salad onto 4 plates. Place in the chops, spoon the marmalade on top and scatter with the remaining rosemary.

Tricks of the Trade

In order to cook pork chops fat sides down, on their narrow edges, I recommend doing it one by one, so you can keep them held on their side with tongs and adjust the angles to make sure you brown all the fat. It will take longer, but the results are worth it, and doing more than one at a time can be tricky.

When I was a little girl, this was my favorite dinner and my mom made enough of it to serve the six of us. Despite that, I have been quite nervous about including this recipe in the book, because it's not something you see every day. It's boiled sausage and potato stew. But, if you think about the concept of some white continental stews in the traditional European canon, such as veal blanquette, coddle is not a million miles away. So I tried making it again from my mother's recipe... and I still think it's my favorite dinner!

I also love that it's simple, and that I'm including a dish from my childhood here, alongside the cauliflower purées, white chocolate creams and so on.

You know how people argue about certain cherished dishes from their countries? A Frenchman might argue with another about the correct ingredients for cassoulet, for instance, while voices have been raised about the right ingredients to include in—and exclude from—a bolognese ragù. Well, there are three types of coddle in Ireland: brown coddle, red coddle (sacrilege!) and—as far as I am concerned—real coddle, which happens to be white. I'm not going to be politically correct about this: the others are wrong. And if anyone has a problem with that, they can talk to my mam.

CODDLE

SERVES 4 GENEROUSLY

1½ tablespoons salted butter
4 thick smoked bacon rashers, snipped with scissors into strips, or 1½ oz (40 g) smoked lardons
1 garlic clove, sliced
1 onion, sliced
2 carrots, chopped
about 1 lb 12 oz (800 g) potatoes, peeled and quartered
2 thyme sprigs
8 sausages, skinned and halved
1¼ cups (300 ml) whole milk, plus more if needed
3 tablespoons heavy cream (optional)
1 teaspoon sea salt
heaped 1 cup (150 g) frozen peas
leaves from ½ bunch of parsley, chopped

Heat up a Dutch oven or heavy pot and add your butter. Sweat off (cook without coloring) your bacon and garlic for 2 minutes, then add the onion and cook for a further 5 minutes.

Now add the carrots, potatoes and thyme and cover halfway with water (about 1¼ cups/300 ml, depending on the size of your dish). Cover with a lid (this helps cook the potatoes that are not covered in water) and cook at a simmer for 20 minutes. You should be able to slide a knife easily into a potato once it's ready.

Add your sausages and simmer for 5 minutes, then pour in the milk and cream, if using, add the salt and taste for seasoning. If your potatoes are very fluffy, they will be really absorbent and you may need more milk.

When you are happy with the flavor, add your peas and parsley and serve, with crusty bread, if you like.

Although my mother is a naturally gifted cook, she didn't always love making dinner every day: being on a tight budget with four grizzly children whining all the time must have been hard work. But dinner was dinner and what was made was all there was available. "Oh, you don't like onion? Tough, it's in there." She was right and I hope I can stick to my guns when Oisín gets older and starts trying to place orders with me at meal times.

So, this pie is a family dinner that my mother made regularly and we all ate without complaining. I'm 100 percent sure that she used whatever ground meat she had in the fridge, or could afford that week. It all tastes good.

What makes this recipe much easier is that, instead of having to make smooth mash, you just boil baby potatoes in their skins and crush them with a fork. This slices the effort in half and gives great texture, too.

MAMMY'S SHEPHERD'S PIE WITH FORKED SPUDS

Boil the potatoes in salted water until you can slide a small knife easily through. Drain them, return them to the pot and add the butter and warmed milk. Using a fork, crush the potatoes with the skins still on, adding a little extra salt.

Now brown the ground meat. This is the most important stage of the recipe and you should give yourself the time to do it right.

Pour 1 tablespoon of the oil into a frying pan and set the pan over medium-high heat. Add half the ground meat, stir and wait 3–5 minutes for the meat to become brown on the bottom before turning it over, breaking it up, then leaving it to color on the other side. Then tip it into a sieve over a bowl and allow the fat to drain away.

Add a splash of water to the pan to deglaze the delicious meat juices off the bottom, pour this into a bowl, then wipe the pan with a tea towel or paper towels and put it back over the heat.

1 lb 12 oz (800 g) baby potatoes
7 tablespoons (100 g) salted
    butter
scant ½ cup (100 ml) milk,
    warmed
4 tablespoons vegetable oil
1 lb 2 oz (500 g) ground lamb,
    ground beef or even ground
    pork
2 garlic cloves, crushed
3 onions, grated or finely chopped
2 carrots, grated or finely
    chopped
¾ cup (175 ml) red wine
1¼ cups (300 ml) chicken stock,
    or water
3 thyme sprigs, plus a few more
    thyme leaves
1½ cups (200 g) frozen peas
1 tablespoon all-purpose flour
2 tablespoons water
sea salt

Repeat with another 1 tablespoon of oil and the second half of the ground meat. Although this process is going to take a longer time than doing it all in one go, the caramelized ground meat will have the best flavor you can get and it's only a little extra effort.

Set a large Dutch oven or heavy pot over medium heat and add the remaining 2 tablespoons of vegetable oil. Add the garlic and cook for 2–5 minutes, then add the onions and cook for 5 minutes. Tip in the browned ground meat and its juices from the bowl, then add the carrots, red wine and stock or water, throw in the thyme and cook for as long as you can, up to 2 hours, if possible. Throw in the peas. Mix the flour in a small bowl with the measured water and stir into the sauce to thicken it. Turn off the heat.

Meanwhile, preheat the oven to 425°F (220°C).

Tip the meat mixture into an oven dish, about 10 in (25 cm) in diameter, or the equivalent.

Carefully top the meat with the forked potatoes. You want them to cover the meat as much as possible. It will help if the meat is chilled before you attempt this, if you have time.

Sprinkle with the extra thyme and put it into the oven to get a little color on top, about 25 minutes. Serve when piping hot all the way through (see below).

The skewer test: pies

First look at the outside of the pie: is it the color you want? If your answer is yes, take its temperature.

There are two ways to do this. The first is with a thermometer: place it in the center of the pie but try not to touch the cooking dish itself, as its temperature will give a reading hotter than that of the food. For meat and fish dishes, or reheated dishes, you are looking for a temperature of 150°F (68°C) and above.

If you do not have a thermometer, do not worry. Take a metal skewer, or thin pointed paring knife, and place it in the center of your pie. Now this time you *do* want to touch the bottom of the dish. Place your thumb on the skewer where the top of the pie is, take the skewer out and quickly place it on the inside of your wrist for a quick second. If it is so hot you cannot leave it there, your dish is piping hot.

Though what were once cheap cuts of meat are now expensive, beef cheek—when it's cooked right—is pure pleasure. If you treat it correctly, it's worth more than any filet mignon, in my book.

This dish is perfect for a birthday dinner, along with a good bottle of wine. Yes, it takes time, but it doesn't need your full attention. I recommend setting a timer and going for a nap, watching TV, enjoying a glass of that wine, or doing whatever else you fancy, while you wait for it to be ready.

BRAISED OX CHEEKS WITH SWEET POTATO & BASIL CRUSH

SERVES 4

FOR THE BEEF
2 ox cheeks (total weight
   2 lb 3 oz/1 kg), each cut in half
3 tablespoons vegetable oil
2 cups (500 ml) red wine
3½ cups (800 ml) chicken
   stock or beef stock, with no
   added salt
2 banana shallots, halved
2 large carrots, left whole
4 garlic cloves, halved
2 tablespoons sugar
2 thyme sprigs
1 large bay leaf
2 tablespoons cornstarch
   (optional)
3 tablespoons water (optional)
sea salt and freshly ground
   black pepper

FOR THE SWEET POTATO
1 lb 12 oz (800 g) sweet potatoes
7 tablespoons (100 g) salted
   butter
1 garlic clove, halved
splash of white wine vinegar
handful of basil leaves, ripped
½ teaspoon sea salt, or to taste

Heat up a frying pan. Sprinkle the ox cheeks with salt and pepper, then fry in the oil, turning, until all sides are golden brown. This should take 5 minutes on each side. Place in a Dutch oven or heavy pot and pour in your wine and stock.

Set over medium heat and bring to a boil, skimming off any foam that rises to the top. Add the vegetables, sugar, thyme and bay leaf, reduce the heat to a simmer, cover and cook for 3–4 hours.

Meanwhile, preheat the oven to 400°F (200°C). Place the sweet potatoes on a baking sheet and bake for 1 hour, or until tender. When cool enough to handle, scoop the sweet potato flesh out of the skins. Melt the butter in a sauté pan and add the garlic. When the garlic browns, lift it out and discard. Put the sweet potato flesh in the pan of garlicky butter with the vinegar and basil and crush with a fork. Add the salt and taste to check the seasoning.

Once the meat is tender, it will feel soft—tender enough that you can easily put a fork through it—and should glisten. Lift the beef out, add an extra sprinkle of salt to it and cover with foil while you finish the sauce.

Remove the vegetables from your cooking liquid and pass the liquid through a sieve. Put it back into the Dutch oven or heavy pot and boil until you have sauce bursting with flavor, with a thick consistency. If you feel it isn't thick enough, mix the cornstarch with the measured water in a small bowl until smooth and gradually add it, stirring all the time. (You might not need it all, so take care.) Taste the sauce and adjust the seasoning.

Serve the sweet potato crush under the ox cheeks, with the sauce poured over the meat.

If you—like me—think filet mignon is overrated, then this recipe might be right up your alley. The black garlic purée takes the most effort, but it really is something. (Ideally, look for jet-black garlic cloves for this.)

Slow-roasted regular garlic is a good alternative (see page 168), if you can't find black garlic.

SIRLOIN STEAKS WITH CHARRED SPROUTING BROCCOLI & BLACK GARLIC

SERVES 2

FOR THE STEAKS AND MARINADE
2 garlic cloves, sliced
leaves from 1 rosemary sprig,
    finely chopped
2 tablespoons olive oil
2 × 7 oz (200 g) sirloin steaks
sea salt

FOR THE BLACK GARLIC PURÉE
1 tablespoon vegetable oil
1 garlic clove, sliced
7 oz (200 g) cremini mushrooms,
    sliced
cloves from ½ black garlic bulb
scant 1 cup (200 ml) chicken
    stock
scant ½ cup (100 ml) heavy
    cream

FOR THE BROCCOLI
6 purple-sprouting broccoli
    spears, or regular broccoli
1 tablespoon extra virgin olive oil
leaves from ½ bunch of tarragon,
    chopped, plus leaves from
    2 sprigs (optional) to serve

Place the garlic, rosemary and olive oil in a bowl, add the steaks, turning to coat, cover and marinate for at least 1 hour.

To make the black garlic purée, heat the oil in a pot. Add the garlic and mushrooms and cook for 3–4 minutes. Add the black garlic and stock and bring to a boil. Once the mushrooms are cooked, add the cream and blend to a purée (see page 181).

Remove the steaks from the marinade, season with salt and cook on a hot griddle pan for 2–3 minutes on each side, depending on size and thickness. Leave to rest in a dish while you prepare the rest of the recipe.

Meanwhile, for the charred sprouting broccoli, heat a griddle pan. If the broccoli spears are tender, char straight away on the hot griddle pan, turning to char all sides. If they are quite tough, blanch them in boiling water first for 3 minutes, then char.

Slice the steaks, adding any additional juices to the broccoli. Toss the charred broccoli with the steak juices, the olive oil and tarragon.

Spoon the black garlic purée onto serving plates, add the steak slices and finish with the sprouting broccoli. Sprinkle with the extra tarragon, if you like, and serve.

Colors

The eye is programmed to understand which colors look attractive together. When we see complementary colors together, we like them, but without consciously considering this while planning your plates, you might not know you know! Here is an easy color spectrum: all the colors that are directly opposite each other are the most complementary.

Take red and green, for instance. When you serve rare steak with bright green broccoli, they make each other look better because they contrast. Similarly, any lemon dessert looks good served with blueberries. It's also a wonderful serendipity that these ingredients not only look great when paired up, through their contrast of colors, but also taste amazing together.

The skewer test: meat

Take your meat out of the oven and put a skewer into the top middle of the protein, touching the base of the pan or plate it is resting on. Leave for 10 seconds, making sure you hold your thumb on the skewer at the top of where the protein is, then remove the skewer and place it on the inside of your wrist. This is something you must get a feel for and isn't as tricky as you think, once you do it a few times. I would recommend, the first time, check the heat of your meat every 2 minutes and feel the temperature rise on your wrist, resulting in you instinctively teaching yourself.

Cold =
undercooked =
below 124°F (51°C)

Cool-warm =
rare =
124–127°F (51–53°C)

Warmer =
medium-rare =
132–135°F (56–57°C)

Hot =
medium =
138–140°F (59–60°C)

Too hot to leave there =
medium-well =
155–158°F (68–70°C)

If you want super-well-done meat, but don't want it bone dry, opt for medium-well and then rest your meat, usually for half the amount of time it took to cook. Then finish it by putting it back into the oven for a further one-quarter of the cooking time. If in doubt, shave a little slice off and see if you like the color. Remember: you are cooking food that *you* want to eat, so cook it as you feel is right.

When I was a kid, Mam always made a traditional Irish stew and I loved it. However, she and my father would argue over what version of Irish stew was correct; he always claimed that it should be made with beef, not lamb, and wanted to add pearl barley, or red lentils.

When I grew up, I discovered the delight of adding red wine to a beef braise and how incredible and different that made it, rendering it unctuous and bursting with flavor. It reminded me of those overheard parental discussions about what should go in authentic Irish stew and, together, both dishes are the inspiration for this recipe.

BOEUF BOURGUIGNON

SERVES 4

olive oil
1 lb 2 oz (500 g) diced stew beef
2¾ tablespoons salted butter, plus more to serve
4 garlic cloves, chopped
1 onion, finely chopped
3 thyme sprigs
3½ oz (100 g) thick smoked lardons, or smoked bacon rashers, chopped
1 cinnamon stick
1 cup (250 ml) red wine
2½ cups (600 ml) beef stock
3 carrots, chopped
1 tablespoon cornstarch (optional)
3 tablespoons water (optional)
1 teaspoon sugar (optional)
3 scallions, thinly sliced at an angle
2 handfuls of kale leaves, coarse ribs removed, chopped
sea salt and freshly ground black pepper

Heat a generous splash of oil in a large frying pan over medium-high heat. Season the beef, then, working in batches, color it on all sides. Using a perforated spoon, transfer each batch to a plate.

Put the butter and garlic in a Dutch oven or heavy pot and cook until very light brown, then add the onion and sweat (cook over low heat without color) for 5–10 minutes. Add the thyme and bacon and stir for 5 minutes, then throw in the cinnamon and beef. Pour in your wine and boil until the liquid reduces by half. Add the stock and bring to a boil, then reduce the heat, cover and simmer for 2 hours, stirring occasionally. It must be gently bubbling, as that is what shows the meat is tenderizing. Add your carrots, cover and cook for 40 minutes, until the beef is meltingly tender.

Taste: if your broth is bursting with flavor but not thick, mix the cornstarch and measured water in a small bowl until smooth and gradually add it, stirring all the time. (You might not need it all, so take care.) If the sauce is too mild, ladle some of the liquid out and reduce it by half, before returning it to the rest of the stew. If it still tastes bland, add a pinch of salt and the sugar.

Finish with the scallions, kale and a few cubes of butter. Cook just until the kale wilts, then serve with creamy mash.

Tricks of the Trade

Getting a lovely golden brown color on the meat is key. Make sure you cook the garlic in fat before adding your onion and then herbs; this gives a great flavor even though it seems too easy to be true. Lastly, make sure you have a good balance of acidity (from wine), sweetness (from vegetables) and a depth of flavor both from how reduced your stock is and from herbs and spices.

Years ago, when my sister Sarah got engaged, I was starting out as a chef, working in a restaurant called L'Ecrivain in Dublin. My sister put me in charge of making a chile con carne for everyone at her engagement party. I had never made chile con carne before, so I found a recipe in the newspaper, bought all the ingredients and followed the recipe to a "T." To my horror, it tasted of nothing. My blood ran cold. I was very young and big sister's approval was the be-all and end-all for me. (It still is: when either of my sisters compliment my cooking today, it still feels like an achievement!) I turned to the restaurant's very talented then-sous chef, Stephen Gibson, with all the fear and panic in my eyes. He tasted the chile and said, "Yeah, that's not going to cut it." He then gave me a masterclass in the fixing of recipes: more chile, more cumin and more paprika went in. More sugar, more salt, then vinegar was added. At the end of it, the chile tasted out of this world. I got lots of praise and approval from my big sisters and their friends, but I gained so much more from that experience. I really learned that a recipe can only be a guideline: you must taste your food and think, at every stage, of what you can add to make a dish sing.

This is a big recipe for a lot of food, that you can make to serve to the family, then portion up the rest in the freezer for a homemade meal to keep on hand.

The slow-roasted bulb of garlic is one of my favorite tricks and it really makes this dish shine.

CHILE CON CARNE

Preheat the oven to 400°F (200°C).

Place the garlic bulb on a piece of foil large enough to wrap it up, pour over 1 tablespoon of the oil and seal the foil around it in a parcel. Place on a baking sheet and roast for 30 minutes.

In a large pot, fry both types of ground meat—in small batches so as not to overcrowd the pot—over high heat. Wait 3–5 minutes for the meat to become brown on the bottom before turning it over, breaking it up, then leaving it to color on the other side. Then tip it into a sieve over a bowl and allow the fat to drain away.

Heat the remaining olive oil in the original large saucepan and add the spices and oregano, frying for a minute or so until they are aromatic. (Some people will tell you to scorch, then soak,

1 garlic bulb, plus 1 garlic clove
4 tablespoons olive oil
1 lb 2 oz (500 g) ground pork
1 lb 2 oz (500 g) ground beef
1½ tablespoons sweet smoked
   paprika
1 cinnamon stick
2 tablespoons cumin seeds
2 dried Mexican chiles, such
   as chipotle
1 teaspoon dried oregano
2 red onions, chopped
2 carrots, chopped
1 red chile, finely chopped
bunch of cilantro, stems finely
   chopped, leaves separated
4 tablespoons tomato paste
3 × 14 oz (400 g) cans of plum
   tomatoes
14 oz (400 g) can of kidney beans,
   drained
2 teaspoons salt, or to taste
2 teaspoons sugar, or to taste
1 tablespoon red wine vinegar,
   or to taste

TO SERVE
boiled rice
sour cream
lime wedges

dried Mexican chiles. I've never bothered with any of that and my chile always tastes great, so throw the chile in whole, just as it comes.)

Now chop the remaining garlic clove, add it to the spices and cook until you can smell that, too. Add the red onions and carrots and cook until the onions have softened and started to become sweet. Don't rush this, as properly cooked onions will elevate the final dish.

Now stir in the chopped fresh chile and the chopped cilantro stems. Tip in the browned ground meat from its sieve, then the tomato paste and the canned tomatoes. Bring to a boil, then reduce the heat to a simmer and cook for 2 hours at a gentle bubble, stirring now and then, or until the meat has become very tender.

Squeeze in the roasted garlic cloves, discarding the papery skins, then add the kidney beans.

Taste the chile and add the salt, sugar and vinegar, tasting once more and adding more salt, sweetness or acidity until you are happy with the balance of the dish.

Scatter the ripped cilantro leaves on top, or serve in a bowl alongside for people to help themselves. Boiled rice, a bowl of sour cream and another of lime wedges are essentials here.

Tricks of the Trade

This recipe will work with whatever ground meat you want to use: lamb, pork or even chicken. However, if you are making it with grounnd chicken, cook for just one hour after you add the canned tomatoes.

Weekend Projects

Yes, cooking is my job, but I'm incredibly lucky that it's also my hobby, born out of passion and curiosity. For instance, I often make a recipe from a country whose food I'm not familiar with, purely because I want to know how it works and to see if I can do it. I also enjoy a recipe which is a bit of a labor of love, or fancier than a quick weeknight supper.

There is evidence to show that, when we complete a mental challenge (such as following a recipe), we create a type of "train track" in our brain, making it easier next time we perform similar challenges. So when you give a recipe a try—even if it might not turn out as expected—feel empowered that you are laying the tracks to becoming a great cook. We do not learn from what we do right; we learn from mistakes, so celebrate the trying and doing as much as the final product.

It's people who enjoy the cooking, or the doing of any other kitchen task, that make the tastiest food. So in this chapter I've shared some more demanding recipes, which I hope will give you great pleasure. They are all worth the extra effort and will give you a real sense of achievement.

One obvious project is the celebration roast dinner. Most of us have at least one occasion a year when we have to cook a big meal, and it can be daunting, so I've offered a timetable for it. But scribble on that to make notes of what works for you, because, hopefully, you will go back time and again to make it as your family's festive meal.

When I started to cook for myself at home as an adult, even though I was a professional chef by then, it was as though I had to re-learn how to cook in a home kitchen! As a professional, you are drilled in skills and techniques and are so focused on those "rules." Cooking at home has taught me so much about adding real flavor by simple means. And I promise you, though the word "consommé" might sound tricky, this is a recipe that you can easily nail.

When you have hung the gazpacho to get a beautiful clear consommé, it is delicious and refreshing as a cold soup in the summer time. This is a dish that just screams hot weather. Ideally, avoid making it in the winter, as the tomatoes won't be as good and they will also be more expensive.

Now, as you embark on this ludicrously simple and elegant recipe, it's very good to note that you can get more than one meal from the dish. It is THE (yes THE) most flavorful stock for risotto or a sauce. And if that's not enough, the consommé makes a great base for a tomato martini. But the real surprise is all the pulp that is left inside the cloth... All the maceration gives it an astounding flavor. Plus, it's hugely satisfying that this is a double-bubble, no-waste dish. Yes, I think on balance this recipe is well worth a whirl!

GAZPACHO CONSOMMÉ
WITH GAZPACHO SALSA CRACKERS

Pulse all the ingredients for the consommé except the basil leaves (but including their stalks) in a food processor.

Take a sieve or conical strainer, line it with a piece of muslin or cheesecloth and place over a large bowl. Pour your consommé mix into the lined sieve or strainer.

Take some string and use it to close up the cloth into a bag, tying it to secure. Attach the string to the middle of a wooden spoon. Balance the wooden spoon across 2 items of the same height, so the wrapped bundle hangs above the bowl. This will drain the maximum amount of liquid. Leave to drip for 1 hour, or as much as overnight, if you're super-organized. You can squeeze the bag if you want, though this will result in a more pinkish gazpacho rather than a clearer liquid, so do try to resist the temptation if you can!

FOR THE CONSOMMÉ

1 lb 9 oz (700 g) tomatoes on
   the vine
scant ½ cup (100 ml) tomato juice
½ cucumber, peeled (peel
   discarded) and chopped
1 garlic clove
1 red pepper, chopped
½ red onion, chopped
3½ tablespoons extra virgin olive
   oil, plus more to serve
4 teaspoons white wine vinegar,
   or to taste
1½ tablespoons sugar, or to taste
1 teaspoon sea salt, or to taste
bunch of basil, leaves and
   stalks separated, stalks
   finely chopped

FOR THE SALSA AND CRACKERS

2 tablespoons cream cheese
1 red chile, finely chopped, plus
   a few slices to serve
1 medium baguette
2 tablespoons extra virgin olive oil
freshly cracked black pepper
a few tomato slices

Carefully remove the bundle from the spoon handle and unwrap it. There is now treasure inside! Mix some of the pulp from the bag with the cream cheese and chile to taste, then cover and set this salsa aside. Put it in the fridge if you are making this ahead of time. Reserve the remaining pulp for another dish (see below).

Cover the consommé and place it in the fridge to chill.

Now for the crackers. Preheat the oven to 340°F (170°C).

Cut the baguette into thin slices and place them on a roasting pan. Drizzle with the oil and cracked pepper and place in the oven to crisp up for 5 minutes. Leave to cool; they will crisp up further.

Now taste the chilled consommé and adjust the seasonings. This is the time to tweak the levels of vinegar, sugar and salt until the balance is perfect for you, as chilling will have blunted the flavors and you will also be serving it chilled.

Serve the chilled consommé in chilled bowls or glasses topped with a drizzle of extra virgin olive oil and a few basil leaves, with the crackers topped with the gazpacho salsa and tomato and chile slices on the side.

Tricks of the Trade

The extra vegetable mixture left inside the cloth is perfectly balanced and makes a showstopping pasta sauce for the next day, especially if you add a dash of cream or tomato passata. Or whizz it up into a dip to have with crudités for lunch...

I first made this recipe out of pure curiosity, as I'd seen versions around and thought I'd give it a whirl. I noticed that if you baked focaccia at a high temperature—which is the norm for bread—the decorations on top burn. So I cranked the oven to a relatively moderate 425°F (220°C) with a very heavy metal pan inside, then put my focaccia on the pan to give it a shock and immediately reduced the oven temperature to 350°F (180°C): the high heat of the pan helps it to rise beautifully and gives you a lovely soft bread with a little crunch. When it comes to decoration, let your imagination run wild. Leftovers and raw veg trimmings all have a role to play.

UNFORGETTABLE FOCACCIA

SERVES 8

¼ oz (7 g) envelope instant yeast
1½ tablespoons sugar
2⅓ cups (550 ml) warm water
6¼ cups (750 g) strong white
    bread flour
2 tablespoons table salt, or
    1 tablespoon kosher salt
2½ tablespoons extra virgin olive
    oil, plus more for drizzling and
    kneading

FOR DECORATION (OPTIONAL)
long chives and other herb sprigs
carrot shavings or peelings
cherry tomatoes
red and yellow peppers, sliced
red onions, sliced
sea salt flakes and freshly cracked
    black pepper

The night before you want to eat the bread, mix the yeast and sugar in a bowl with a few tablespoons of the measured warm water. Leave for 10–15 minutes, until it foams on the surface.

Put the flour and salt in a large bowl, make a well in the center, then pour in the yeast mix with the remaining measured warm water and mix with your hands until it forms a dough. Tip the dough out onto an oiled work surface. It should be a wet and sticky dough and difficult to handle, as this gives a soft, moist bread: the drier it is, the longer it takes to proof. Oil your hands with the olive oil, to stop the dough from sticking to your fingers, then knead it with a drop more of whatever oil you have.

Line a tray with plastic and coat with oil to prevent the base of the dough from drying and creating a skin. Place the dough on top and rub with a little more oil, then cover with a damp tea towel and leave in the fridge to proof slowly overnight. This will give you a lovely sourdough tang. It should double in size.

Line a baking dish measuring 12 x 8 in (30 × 20 cm)—and which has some depth to it—with parchment paper. Once your dough is proofed, knock it back and put into the dish, pressing it out with your fingertips until it lies evenly in the dish. Cover with a damp tea towel once more and let it proof for another 10–20 minutes.

Preheat the oven to 425°F (220°C) and place a larger baking sheet inside; you'll set your focaccia on top of it, to give a better bake. Use your chosen decorations to create a design on top of the dough. (Then remove any green stuff until after it has baked.)

Place the bread on the large baking sheet in the oven, reduce the oven temperature to 350°F (180°C) and bake for 30 minutes. When it comes out, return the green bits to create your piece of art, then scatter with sea salt flakes and black pepper.

Many many years ago, when I still lived in Dublin, I flew over to London for a weekend, especially to eat at a restaurant called Pied à Terre where Shane Osborn was the head chef. The meal was absolutely fantastic. My appetizer was a pressed duck leg and foie gras terrine with a delicate, perfectly picked frisée salad. When I ate the salad, I thought: "I have to work here one day, to learn how to make something so simple but which leaves such an impression." So that very humble dressing inspired me to get a job working with Shane Osborn.

This is a salad that is intended to be served at room temperature or cold, which makes it relaxing to put together, to take your time and enjoy the process.

You only need 3½ tablespoons of vinaigrette here, but this recipe makes more than that. It's great to keep in the fridge for adding to salads or veggies, as you need. (Make sure you shake up the jar of dressing before weighing it out, so each portion you use always has the right ratio of oil to vinegar.)

Any extra pickled raisins will stay good for a week or two and are brilliant used as a secret weapon to throw into salads.

CARROT, PICKLED RAISIN & HAZELNUT SALAD WITH AIRING-CUPBOARD VINAIGRETTE

To make the vinaigrette, put your shallot and garlic in a bowl or jar and sprinkle with a pinch of salt. Add both types of oil and then the vinegar and herbs. Cover the bowl with plastic, or seal the jar, and leave somewhere warm, such as in an airing cupboard or above the oven, for a minimum of 30 minutes, but ideally 3 days. Yes, it sounds like a fuss, but trust me this dressing will get better and better each day until day 5. Then you must pour it through a sieve, add the sugar and mustard and whisk to emulsify, seal it in a jar and keep it in the fridge.

For the carrot purée, put the carrots in a pot, then pour in water to come halfway up to the level of the carrots (3½ tablespoons should do it). Add the butter, star anise, sugar and a pinch of salt, cover and set over medium-high heat. Cook it for 5 minutes, then check to see if the carrot is soft. If it is, purée it (see right) with the buttery liquid, removing the star anise, or leaving the spice in there too if you're looking for a stronger flavor.

Now for the raisins. Bring the measured water, vinegar and a pinch of salt to a boil in a saucepan. Add the raisins and cook

FOR THE VINAIGRETTE
1 shallot, thickly sliced
1 garlic clove, halved
3½ tablespoons olive oil
scant ½ cup (100 ml) vegetable
   oil
⅓ cup (75 ml) white wine vinegar
1 thyme sprig
1 rosemary sprig
1 tablespoon sugar
1 teaspoon Dijon mustard
sea salt

FOR THE CARROT PURÉE
7 oz (200 g) carrots, peeled and
   grated
3½ tablespoons salted butter
1 star anise
pinch of sugar

FOR THE PICKLED RAISINS
3½ tablespoons water
3½ tablespoons white wine
   vinegar
⅓ cup (50 g) raisins

FOR THE CARROT STRIPS
1 carrot, ideally purple

FOR THE TARRAGON MAYONNAISE
1 tablespoon breadcrumbs
2 tablespoons water
1 tablespoon Dijon mustard
1 tablespoon white wine vinegar
½ garlic clove, crushed
leaves from ½ bunch of tarragon,
   plus more to serve
scant ½ cup (100 ml) vegetable
   oil

FOR THE CARROT SALAD
3 large carrots, in different colors,
   if you want
⅓ cup (50 g) toasted hazelnuts,
   chopped

for 1 minute over low heat. Transfer to a small container and leave to soak.

For the carrot strips, take a peeler and peel your carrot. Then continue to peel long strips of carrot and place in a bowl, sprinkling with a pinch of salt. The salt will not only flavor the strips, but will draw out the water and make them more pliable. Wrap the strips of carrot around your finger, to create tubes.

To make the mayonnaise, soak the breadcrumbs in a blender jug in the measured water for 20 minutes. Add the mustard, vinegar and garlic and blend until smooth. Now add the tarragon and blend on high speed until you have a smooth green paste. On medium-low speed, gradually add the vegetable oil. Season with salt.

For the salad, slice the carrots at an angle about ⅛ in (5 mm) thick, then boil them in salted water until cooked but still with a bite to them. Check after 3 minutes, but they might take as much as 6. Drain them. If you are serving the salad straight away, refresh them under cold running water to cool them down. Dress them in 3½ tablespoons of the vinaigrette.

Place the purée on plates, spoon the dressed carrot on top, then sprinkle with hazelnuts and pickled raisins (don't use their pickling liquid, though). Add the ribbons of raw carrot, splashes of the tarragon mayonnaise and a sprinkling of tarragon leaves, then serve.

Tricks of the Trade

Unlike blending (see page 37), puréeing is when you are looking for silky-smooth texture, such as here, to complement the rest of a dish. You need a jug blender, or sometimes a hand blender. You want to continuously blend the mixture, checking it every 2–3 minutes to see how silky-smooth it is. If it is not smooth, there are three main reasons: there's not enough liquid; the vegetables were not fully cooked; or you don't have enough mixture for the blender to connect with to purée it properly.

Once you've made this recipe for the first time, you can create so many different varieties based on it. You can use ground chicken, any ground meat you have or black pudding instead of sausage meat. Then change it up with different herbs, or add nuts and seeds if you want.

If you don't have bacon, wrap your stuffed chicken breast in foil and it will work like a dream cooked in the same way. (Though remove the foil before cutting!)

I recommend making an extra couple of rosti, as they are very delicious, even when served cold.

STUFFED & ROAST CHICKEN BREAST WITH POTATO ROSTI

SERVES 2

FOR THE STUFFED CHICKEN
3½ oz (100 g) sausage meat (or see recipe introduction)
¼ teaspoon freshly ground black pepper
leaves from ½ bunch of parsley, chopped
leaves from 2–3 thyme sprigs
2 skinless chicken breasts
8 thinly sliced rashers of smoked bacon

FOR THE ROSTI
2 potatoes, unpeeled, parboiled for 10 minutes
2 tablespoons vegetable oil
1 garlic clove, halved
sea salt

TO SERVE
sour cream
wilted spinach

Put the sausage meat in a bowl and season with the pepper, then fold in the chopped parsley and thyme leaves.

Put the chicken breasts on a work surface and slice horizontally, lengthways, to create pockets. Fill with the sausage mix.

Preheat the oven to 410°F (210°C).

Lay 4 bacon rashers next to each other. Lay a chicken breast on one end of the bacon, then roll it up. Repeat to wrap and secure the second chicken breast in the remaining bacon. Wrap both in foil and place them, spaced well apart, on a roasting pan.

Pop in the oven for 10 minutes, then turn and cook for another 10 minutes. Remove from the oven and allow the chicken to rest, in the foil, for 5 minutes. Unwrap the chicken breasts: if they need some color, give them a quick sear in a separate frying pan as you're cooking the rosti, then leave to rest for another few minutes.

Meanwhile, make the rosti. Grate the parboiled potatoes on a box grater—no need to peel—and season them with salt.

Heat a frying pan over medium heat with the oil. Cover the pan with the rosti, flatten it out, then slowly let it turn crisp and golden brown. Flip it over and let the other side cook. This won't take long, as your potatoes are parcooked. When both sides are golden brown, throw in the halved garlic clove and cook for 3 minutes.

Once your chicken has rested, slice and serve with wedges of your rosti, with a dollop of sour cream and some spinach, drizzling any chicken resting juices over the meat.

The first time I cooked duck was when I was a commis chef studying Professional Cookery at Cathal Brugha Street in Dublin. My mother could see how passionate I was about cooking, so she would take me to the supermarket twice a month to choose some ingredients I wanted to learn to cook with. I remember researching juniper berries and we went to every single food shop in the Square in Tallaght—the local mammoth mall—searching for them. I think we eventually found them in a health food shop on the ground level and they weren't cheap. I was blown away by the smell (and was yet to really discover gin and tonic). As I write, I do understand that some ingredients are not easy to find these days and sometimes can be surprisingly expensive, too. What I will say is that every ingredient should be cherished and you should always try to get the most out of them.

We all get stuck doing the same things with potatoes (mash or fries), and although both are yummy it's also nice to think outside the box and do something different, such as these waffles.

ROASTED JUNIPER-MARINATED DUCK & POTATO WAFFLE

Mix your crushed juniper berries and rosemary with your oil and a sprinkling of pepper. Place your duck breasts skin-side down on a plate and rub this marinade only on the red flesh. Cover and put in the fridge until you are ready to cook.

Peel the potatoes, place them in a pot of cold water and bring to a boil. Once the potatoes are thoroughly cooked (you should easily be able to slide a knife in), drain them and push through a potato ricer to make a dry mash.

Mix all the waffle ingredients together, including the duck fat or olive oil, then cook in a waffle machine for 4 minutes, or according to the manufacturer's instructions. Set aside. Now although this recipe asks for a waffle iron, don't worry if you don't have one, as you can also choose to shape the mix into squares and fry them over medium heat in a frying pan with 3 tablespoons of vegetable oil instead.

Now for the mushroom sauce. Sweat the finely sliced regular garlic cloves off in the butter in a sauté pan. Add the sliced mushrooms and the black garlic and cook for 5 minutes. Pour in your stock, bring to a boil and simmer for 10 minutes. Now pour in the cream, return the pan to a boil, then purée until

FOR THE DUCK

1 teaspoon juniper berries, crushed
leaves from 1 rosemary sprig,
    chopped
2 tablespoons vegetable oil
2 duck breasts
3 garlic cloves, halved
1 large fennel bulb, chopped
sea salt and freshly cracked
    black pepper

FOR THE WAFFLES

1 lb 3 oz (550 g) Russet potatoes
1 teaspoon sea salt
¼ cup (25 g) cornstarch
2 small egg yolks
¼ teaspoon garlic powder
4 teaspoons melted duck fat or
    olive oil

FOR THE MUSHROOM SAUCE

2 garlic cloves, finely sliced
1 tablespoon salted butter
1 lb 2 oz (500 g) cremini
    mushrooms, sliced
6 black garlic cloves
⅔ cup (150 ml) chicken stock
3½ tablespoons heavy cream
scant ½ cup (100 ml) whole milk

FOR THE SALAD

¼ Savoy cabbage, shredded
½ fennel bulb, very finely sliced
handful of parsley leaves
2 tablespoons capers, drained
1 quantity House vinaigrette
    (see page 28)

silky smooth (see page 181), adding ½ teaspoon of salt. Now slowly add the milk until the sauce consistency is as you want it. You're looking for a lovely smooth pouring sauce, with a texture like a silky custard. Make sure your sauce isn't too thin and will work with how you want to present it on the plate.

Once you are ready to cook your duck, preheat the oven to 375°F (190°C).

Use a teaspoon to scrape the juniper and rosemary mixture off the meat. Sprinkle salt on the skin and the flesh of your duck.

Place the duck breasts fat side down in a cold pan, then set it over medium-low heat. This will let the fat melt off, resulting in a crisper skin. It should take about 4 minutes for the skin to start to turn golden brown. Put the halved regular garlic cloves and the fennel in a roasting pan and place the duck breasts on top, fat side up.

Put the duck in the oven for 4–5 minutes (see page 165 for advice on how to cook your meat to the temperature you want). Leave it to rest for 5 minutes.

Meanwhile, make the salad: mix all the vegetables and capers in a bowl, then toss with the vinaigrette.

Slice the duck thickly and serve, with the potato waffles and fennel salad on the side. Serve the sauce on the side, or pour it onto the plates.

Tricks of the Trade

This is a recipe that you want to make on special occasions; it's not your average Monday night dinner. You can make most of it a day or so in advance, however, so the only thing you need to cook in the moment is the duck breast.

When I say I love black pudding, people usually scrunch up their noses and ask, "Sure, what can you use it for?" The answer is that any recipe that calls for chorizo could easily use black pudding instead. It's even more nutritious. When I was a child and we were given a full Irish breakfast, the four of us siblings would negotiate and I would happily swap my bacon or an egg for black pudding. (And absolutely my mushrooms, I was always trying to offload those bad boys.) It was like the Stock Exchange at our house at breakfast time.

I come from a country that has lots of wonderful ingredients and produce on our doorstep and certain of those—carrots, cabbage, the meat of ex-dairy beef and black pudding—we take for granted because we have them in abundance. Black pudding is a byproduct of eating beef or pork; most is pork-based, but I've used a Clonakilty beef pudding in my recipe. You can substitute pork-based black pudding, or any blood sausage if you can't find it.

These parcels are really great to take on a picnic or to work, as a ready-to-go snack. They also make wonderful party food, as you can eat something substantial that fits easily in your hand, serving the apple dip on the side.

BLACK PUDDING PARCELS WITH APPLE DIP & APPLE-BARLEY SALAD

Remove the casing from the black pudding, crumble it into a bowl and add the chicken. Pour in the cream, adding a pinch of salt, then mix well until properly amalgamated. Your hands are the best tool for this and you can wear a food-safe plastic glove if you want.

Brush a sheet of samosa pastry with melted butter or oil. Spoon 1 tablespoon of black pudding mixture in the top right corner of a strip. Brush again with butter or oil, then fold the black pudding-filled top right-hand corner of the strip over to form a triangle. Continue down the strip, folding left to right, in triangles each time, until you reach the end of the strip. This isn't at all difficult and there are lots of videos to show you how online, if you want to take a look before you start.

Secure the end of the samosa pastry, using the butter or oil to "glue" it to the rest of the parcel. Repeat to form all the black pudding parcels.

FOR THE PARCELS

12½ oz (350 g) Clonakilty (beef-based) black pudding, or pork-based black pudding
7 oz (200 g) ground chicken
scant ½ cup (100 ml) heavy cream
6 sheets of samosa pastry
melted butter, or oil, to brush the pastry
sea salt

FOR THE APPLE DIP

1 tart cooking apple, peeled, cored and chopped
1 tablespoon sugar
2 heaped tablespoons cream cheese
juice of ½ lemon
1 tablespoon chopped chives

FOR THE SALAD

generous 1 cup (250 g) cooked pearl barley (⅔ cup/150 g raw, if cooking it yourself)
3 tablespoons extra virgin olive oil
2 tablespoons white wine vinegar
1 teaspoon sugar
1 Granny Smith apple
2–3 tablespoons chopped pecans

TO SERVE

handful of flat-leaf parsley leaves, ripped or finely chopped
¼ head of radicchio, leaves roughly torn

Preheat the oven to 400°F (200°C).

Place the finished black pudding parcels on a roasting pan, leaving plenty of space between each, and drizzle with oil or brush with butter. Cook in the oven for 10 minutes.

To make the apple dip, put the apple in a saucepan with the sugar and place over low heat. Cook the fruit in the apple juices that leak out of it, stirring regularly, until fluffy and soft, then leave to cool. This cooking will happen fairly quickly, and even more rapidly if you cover it with a lid. Mix the cooked apple fluff with the cream cheese, lemon juice and chives.

Meanwhile, make the salad. If cooking your own pearl barley, you will need to boil it in salted water for 15–20 minutes. Pearl barley is cooked when you enjoy chewing it!

Mix together the oil, vinegar, sugar and a pinch of salt, whisking with a fork to emulsify. Grate the Granny Smith apple into a bowl and stir in the cooked barley, then stir in the dressing. This is best made only at the point when you are going to eat it, as the apple needs to be coated with dressing before it oxidizes (turns brown). Scatter with the pecan nuts, to add crunch.

Spoon the apple dip into the center of the plates and make a well in it. Spoon in your pearl barley salad and scatter with the parsley and radicchio leaves. Finish with your black pudding parcels and serve.

As I've been writing for this book about the recipes that mean the most to me, I've been surprised to find how much my father affects the food I love, since my mother is the great cook in our house and taught me so much. Now here we are heading back to Joe Haugh flavor town! My father loves lamb chops. My entire family loves lamb chops. I love lamb chops.

Cauliflower is always a vegetable to be found on my father's plate come dinnertime. In this recipe I really celebrate it, using it as both a charred vegetable and a sauce, and it takes a whole one and a half of them. Already a naturally sweet vegetable, once roasted or caramelized, cauliflower becomes nutty and even more delicious.

A great side to go with your lamb and cauliflower is scrunched kale with toasted seeds: scrunch the kale leaves in a vinaigrette (see pages 28 and 181), massaging it in, then scatter with toasted seeds.

RACK OF IRISH LAMB & DOUBLE CAULIFLOWER

Break the larger natural florets from the cauliflower, then slice each large floret in 3: you want about 6 florets per person, so you need to cut off the 8 biggest florets.

Heat up a frying pan and add the oil. Add your cauliflower florets and color to a hard caramelization—really scorch them on each side—then sprinkle salt on top. Set aside.

Take the rest of the cauliflower including the root (but trim off the woody bit near the end) and chop well. Place in a pot and add your milk, cream and another pinch of salt; the liquids should just reach halfway up the cauliflower. Bring to a boil, then reduce the heat to a low simmer and cook for 5–10 minutes. You should be able to squash a piece of cauliflower against the pot; that's how you know it's ready. Purée until silky-smooth (see page 181), then taste for salt and adjust if needed. Set aside.

Preheat the oven to 375°F (190°C).

Season the lamb racks with salt on all sides, then set aside for 5 minutes while you prepare the carrots. Peel your carrots, slice on an angle about ½ in (1 cm) thick, place in a roasting pan and sprinkle with salt. They will form the base your lamb cooks on, but you will also be eating them. Roast for 5 minutes.

Place your racks of lamb, fat side down, in a cold frying pan. Turn the heat on to medium-low to begin to warm that fat. This allows it to melt away. As it continues to cook, the fat will color

FOR THE CAULIFLOWER
1½ cauliflowers
2 tablespoons vegetable oil
scant ½ cup (100 ml) whole milk
scant ½ cup (100 ml) heavy
    cream
sea salt

FOR THE LAMB
2 × 9 oz (250 g) French-trimmed
    racks of lamb
2 carrots

TO SERVE
7 oz (200 g) baguette, sliced
2 garlic cloves, halved
2 teaspoons extra virgin olive oil,
    plus more for the baguette
handful of chives, chopped
1 tablespoon balsamic vinegar,
    plus more for the purée
1 tablespoon capers

and turn golden brown; when that happens, it's time to get it in the oven.

Place the lamb, fat side up, on top of your par-roasted carrots and cook for 8 minutes, then check whether it is done to your requirements (see page 165 to help you cook the meat to the degree you love). If not, continue to cook the lamb for a total of 10 minutes and check again. Once cooked, let the lamb rest, still on the carrots, for 5 minutes. If you have a kitchen thermometer, use it: for medium-rare, the temperature in the center should be about 117°F/47°C (this will climb after the meat has rested, due to its residual heat, see page 201).

Remove the lamb and place it on a carving board, insulating it by wrapping in foil while you finish the vegetables and sauce. Let it rest for about half the total time it took to cook.

Pop your cauliflower florets into the oven to heat through. Gently reheat your cauliflower purée in a small saucepan, adding the lamb resting juices.

Place the baguette slices on a baking sheet and rub them with the cut side of the garlic cloves, then sprinkle with oil and toast in the oven for 3–5 minutes until golden and crunchy.

Toss your carrots in the chopped chives, the 2 teaspoons of olive oil and the vinegar.

You can carve the rack or leave it whole—for extra wow factor—to serve. Serving the racks whole will also keep the temperature in the meat.

Spoon 4–5 tablespoons of cauliflower purée into a serving dish and place the charred cauliflower florets on top. Scatter with the capers and drizzle with a little balsamic vinegar.

Put a spoon of cauliflower purée on each plate, add the carrots and the lamb, drizzle the carrots with their vinaigrette and serve, with the dish of cauliflower florets on the side.

Tricks of the Trade

You will probably have more cauliflower purée than you need, because you need a certain volume in a blender in order for the blades to process it into a purée. However, the next day, stir in a little more milk, reheat it gently and you have a great soup to eat for lunch, either scattered with cheese or, for a treat, with my Ultimate Cheese & Ham Double Decker Toastie (see page 82).

SPROUT SLAW

1 tablespoon honey
3½ tablespoons white wine
    vinegar
2 lb 3 oz (1 kg) of the biggest
    Brussels sprouts you can find,
    sliced extra finely or grated (or
    see recipe introduction)
scant ½ cup (100 ml) olive oil
½ teaspoon sea salt
1 teaspoon caraway seeds, or
    cumin seeds, or chile flakes,
    or finely sliced red chile
1 teaspoon pink peppercorns,
    crushed

If you can't face slicing 2 lb 3 oz (1 kg) of sprouts, you can slice 1 lb 2 oz (500 g) of them and add 1 lb 2 oz (500 g) of shredded white cabbage. This recipe will also work made entirely with any cabbage, such as Savoy or Hispi. It may sound simple, but my goodness is it one that I believe will permanently stick in your repertoire. It's a Haugh family staple and is excellent with cold cuts the next day in a sandwich. What makes this recipe so lovely is that you can use the spices you love.

Mix the honey into the vinegar in a small cup until smooth, then simply mix all the ingredients together.

GLORIOUS GRAVY

2 tablespoons vegetable oil
2 onions, chopped
2 garlic cloves, crushed
1 cup (250 g) red wine
1 vegetable stock cube
3½ cups (800 ml) boiling water
a couple of thyme sprigs
2 tablespoons all-purpose flour
handful of chopped tarragon
    leaves (optional)
a few pats of butter (optional)

If you have made your gravy ahead of time and frozen it, ideally take it out of the freezer the day before and let it defrost in the fridge overnight, then just bring it up to a boil before serving. It's also vegetarian unless you add any meat juices.

Heat the oil in a deep frying pan over medium heat, add the onions and garlic and cook until golden brown. Pour in the red wine and reduce down by two-thirds.

Meanwhile, dissolve the vegetable stock cube in the measured boiling water.

Add the stock and thyme to the onions and bring to a boil.

In a small bowl or cup, mix the flour with 2 tablespoons of water to make a paste, then mix that into your gravy. Don't add salt yet, because if you're planning to add the juices from a roast, they might be salty, so always wait until you have added those before you adjust the seasoning. Cool the gravy, then freeze, if making ahead.

Bring to a boil, add any resting juices from the meat, then taste and adjust the seasoning to serve. If you like, and it works with your meal, you could whisk in the tarragon and butter just before serving.

STUFFING BALLS

1⅓ cups (150 g) breadcrumbs or
   crushed stale crackers
14 oz (400 g) sausage meat
   (if you want to make this
   vegetarian, use 1¼ cups/
   200 g crushed chickpeas and
   1¾ cups/200 g grated cheese)
1 egg, lightly beaten
fresh herbs (I used the leaves
   from 3 lemon thyme sprigs,
   ½ bunch of parsley and
   10 sage leaves), chopped
2 teaspoons sea salt
3½ tablespoons water
a little oil

*To make your life easier, you should make these ahead,
so they only need to be cooked on the day.*

Mix all the ingredients except the oil together, adding the water
at the end, just when you think you have mixed it all enough
(see page 46). Shape into 25–30 bite-sized balls (you can mix
and form these the day before) and place on a baking sheet.

Preheat the oven to 425°F (220°C). Drizzle the stuffing balls
with oil and roast for 20 minutes.

PIMPED-UP CARROTS

6 extra-large carrots
1 teaspoon sugar
1½ teaspoons sea salt
⅓ cup (100 g) maple syrup
3½ tablespoons Dijon mustard
2 teaspoons cumin seeds,
   crushed
1 teaspoon chile flakes
1 teaspoon coriander seeds,
   crushed
1 teaspoon sesame seeds
palmful of thyme leaves

*While these are just wonderful with a roast dinner,
you can turn them into a dish on their own. Spoon
2 tablespoons of hummus onto a plate, put the carrots
on top with a handful of spinach leaves, scatter on a few
toasted nuts and you have a show-stopping lunch.*

Put your carrots in a large pot of water with the sugar and
1 teaspoon of the salt and cook for 5 minutes, or until you can
slide a knife easily inside them. Run them under cold water to
halt the residual cooking (see page 201), then drain. Cut the
carrots in half lengthways and lay on a baking sheet.

Mix the maple syrup and mustard together. Spoon this glaze
on top of the carrots and sprinkle with ½ teaspoon more salt,
all the spices and seeds and the thyme leaves.

Preheat the oven to 425°F (220°C). Roast for 20 minutes.

This is so full of flavor and texture and satisfaction that I think anyone who doesn't eat meat will be reassured that their dish challenges the more conventional main course. It's worth putting a bit of effort into this, and into making it look good, as it should be celebrated and everyone will enjoy eating it.

You can make this ahead of time, then slice it into thick pieces and sear like a steak to serve. Or you can place the whole loaf back in the oven on a baking sheet lined with parchment paper, cook for 15 minutes, then serve it as a centerpiece.

If you want to make this vegan, remove the eggs, add some extra breadcrumbs and stock and cook the mixture for a little longer in the pan, then bake in the same way.

NUTTYLICIOUS LOAF

SERVES 6

FOR THE LOAF
2 teaspoons fennel seeds
3–4 tablespoons olive oil
4 garlic cloves, crushed
2 teaspoons chopped rosemary
  leaves, plus more to serve
2 teaspoons chopped thyme
  leaves, plus more to serve
2 banana shallots, or small red
  onions, finely chopped
1 cup (200 g) cooked lentils
7 oz (200 g) pumpkin (skinned
  and deseeded weight), grated
1¾ cups (200 g) breadcrumbs
generous 1 cup (100 g) rolled oats
1¼ cups (300 ml) vegetable stock
¾ cup (120 g) toasted hazelnuts
¾ cup (120 g) sunflower seeds
scant ½ cup (60 g) pumpkin seeds
4 eggs, lightly beaten
2 teaspoons sea salt
edible flowers, to serve (optional)

FOR THE GLAZE
1 tablespoon Vegemite, Marmite,
  or Promite (or thick soy sauce
  in a pinch)
1 cup (200 g) sugar
3½ tablespoons white wine
  vinegar
3½ tablespoons water

Preheat the oven to 400°F (200°C) and line a 9½ x 5 in (2 lb/900 g) loaf pan with parchment paper. If your pan is a little rusty, I'd recommend lining it with foil first and then with parchment paper.

Tip the fennel seeds into a dry frying pan, place over medium heat and stir until toasted and fragrant. Immediately tip into a mortar, or a small food processor, and grind to a powder.

Pour the oil into a medium pot, add your garlic and cook for 1 minute until it's almost turning golden brown, then add the herbs and ground fennel seeds and stir until aromatic. Add your shallots or onions and cook for 5–10 minutes over low heat.

Add the lentils, pumpkin, breadcrumbs, oats and stock and cook for a few minutes, stirring to bring the mix together. Make sure everything is well cooked out, then stir in all but a handful of the nuts and seeds.

Tip into a bowl and stir in your eggs well, along with the salt. Press the mixture into your prepared pan, then bake for 35 minutes.

Meanwhile, for the glaze, mix all the ingredients in a saucepan, place over medium-low heat and stir continuously until the sugar has fully dissolved.

Once you are ready to serve, brush the nut loaf with the glaze and scatter with your reserved nuts and seeds and the extra herbs. Add some marigold petals (Irish saffron!) if you like and if they are in season, or chive flowers, then serve.

This chart presumes you have, in advance:
- *Cooked the Nuttylicious loaf,*
- *Made the Stuffing balls and Glorious gravy,*
- *The night before, defrosted your gravy, if needed.*
  GOOD LUCK!

TIMINGS CHART

THE DAY BEFORE   Clear your work space! Make sure work surfaces are clear and clean and put away any clutter. Plan which cookware and servingware you will be using for each dish. If you need to supplement your cookware, buy some recyclable foil trays (these will also help with clean-up afterwards).

BEFORE YOU BEGIN   If you think it's likely that people will be wandering in and out for lemonade, potato chips or wine top-ups, get those things out of the kitchen and into another room.

9AM   Marinate the turkey in the buttermilk, salt, thyme, garlic and lemon zest and juice for 1 hour.

9:30AM   This is a good time to peel your potatoes and carrots if you haven't done that the night before.

Time to make your Sprout slaw. Once it is made, spoon it into your serving dish, cover and place somewhere cool. (We know: there's no space in the fridge today.)

9:45AM   Preheat the oven to 350°F (180°C).

10AM   After an hour of marinating, put the turkey in a large roasting pan and place in the preheated oven for 2½ hours.

11:30AM   Parboil your carrots. Drain and dress with the maple mixture and seeds and place on a roasting pan lined with parchment paper.

12PM   Time to parboil your potatoes.

12.30PM Check the color of your turkey. If needed, increase the oven temperature to 425°F (220°C). Either way, continue to cook for 30 minutes.

Lay your potatoes around the turkey, or roast them on their own pan. Drizzle with the vegetable oil or melted duck fat.

1PM Increase the oven temperature to 425°F (220°C), if you haven't already done so.

Time to check the core temperature of the turkey. It ideally should measure 140°F (60°C) in the center. When the oven is at 425°F (220°C), it will create residual heat (see page 201), so the temperature of the turkey will continue rising as it rests for 1 hour. If the internal temperature is 140°F (60°C), take the turkey out of the oven. If you do not have a kitchen thermometer, you still need to test whether the turkey is cooked. Push a skewer or thin knife into the thickest part: the juices should run clear. If they are pinkish, cook for 15 minutes more, then test again. And do the skewer temperature check, too (see page 113). Either way, when the turkey is ready, wrap it in foil and rest in a dish to catch the cooking juices.

1:15PM Turn your potatoes over and, if they are pale, return them to the oven at the same temperature. If they are golden brown, reduce the temperature of the oven to 400°F (200°C).

1:30PM Place the Pimped-up carrots and Stuffing balls in the oven to roast for 20 minutes.

1:40PM Bring your gravy up to a boil and pour into your gravy boat.

Make the glaze for the Nuttylicious loaf.

Put the cooked Nuttylicious loaf in the oven to reheat.

1:50PM Check your Perfect roast potatoes: if they are done, take them out and pile them high in your serving dish.

2PM Start carving your turkey and plate on a large serving platter with the Stuffing balls, adding any turkey juices to the Glorious gravy pan and then adjusting the seasoning. Brush the turkey slices with the warm lemony butter.

Glaze the Nuttylicious loaf.

Place the carrots in their serving dish, take everything to the table and dig in.

Aunty Ann is my godmother. I have to say our family were blessed that she inherited her Aunty Connie's touch in the kitchen. I have eaten so many dishes made by her hands and have never been in anything but complete bliss with every bite. It was her carrot cake that really rocked my world, with the chunky walnuts on top that add such great texture.

This is a three-layer cake that will turn heads when it is brought into the room. The carrot jam is optional, but a nice touch, and if you make a large amount it's great with The perfect fluffy scones (see page 224) and cream.

AUNTY ANN'S SHOW-STOPPING CARROT CAKE WITH CARROT JAM

Before you start the jam, put a saucer into the fridge or freezer.

To make the jam, put all your ingredients except the lemon juice in a pot and boil for 30 minutes, stirring occasionally. To test the set, you have 2 options. Check on a kitchen thermometer: it is ready when it has reached 220°F (105°C). Or take a small amount of jam and put it on the chilled saucer. (Turn off the heat while testing, to avoid overcooking.) Leave for 5 minutes. Run your finger through the jam: it should hold a strong line where your finger was. If it runs back together, keep cooking for another 10–15 minutes. Whichever test you are using, perform it again and again until the jam is ready to take off the heat. When cool enough, taste the jam, and add the lemon juice if you think it needs it.

Cover the jam and place in the fridge to set before using. This will keep for weeks covered in the fridge.

Now for the cake. Preheat the oven to 400°F (200°C). Oil 3 × 8 in (20 cm) round cake pans and line the bases with parchment paper.

Put your grated carrots in a bowl, add the salt to them and mix well. Stir in your buttermilk. Now mix in your sugar, then beat in the eggs until incorporated. Finally, beat in your oil.

Mix the flour, cinnamon, ginger and baking soda in a large bowl and make a well in the center. Pour the carrot mixture into the well and whisk into a batter.

FOR THE JAM (OPTIONAL)

3 cups (300 g) grated carrots
¾ cup (150 g) jam sugar (this is
    sugar with pectin added,
    see Tricks of the Trade)
3½ tablespoons water
seeds from 2 green cardamom
    pods, crushed
1 cinnamon stick
squeeze of lemon juice (optional)

FOR THE CAKE

2 cups (450 ml) vegetable oil,
    plus more for the pan
4 cups (400 g) grated carrots
½ teaspoon fine sea salt
scant ½ cup (100 ml) buttermilk
2⅓ cups (500 g) brown sugar
5 eggs, lightly beaten
3¾ cups (450 g) all-purpose flour
1 tablespoon ground cinnamon
½ teaspoon ground ginger
2 teaspoons baking soda
¾ cup (100 g) whole walnuts
bunch of mint

FOR THE FROSTING

10 tablespoons (150 g) unsalted
    butter, at room temperature
2⅔ cups (300 g) confectioners'
    sugar
2¼ cups (500 g) cream cheese,
    at room temperature
juice of 1–2 lemons

Pour into the prepared pans and bake for 25 minutes. The cakes are ready when a skewer inserted into the middle emerges clean. (To be doubly sure, the cakes will be ready when they have reached 203–208°F/95–98°C on a kitchen thermometer.) Cool the cakes in their pans for 10 minutes, then remove.

While the cake is baking, make your frosting.

In a stand mixer fitted with the paddle attachment, tip in your room-temperature butter. The butter should be soft enough for your finger to easily slide into it, but not melted in any way. (Or you can also do this with an electric hand mixer and a mixing bowl.)

Beat the butter on a medium-high setting for 1 minute, then reduce the speed to low and spoon in your confectioners' sugar gradually (this is to stop a cloud of confectioners' sugar going everywhere).

Once that is done, you are going to add the cream cheese. It is very important that the cream cheese is at the same room temperature as the rest of the beaten mixture. If it is cold, it will set the butter and the frosting will look split and not have a nice texture. Beat this in gradually, then add the juice of 1 lemon, beat this in too, then check for acidity. Add more lemon juice if you like, until the flavor is right for you. Swirl the carrot jam through the frosting, making sure it is rippled and not mixed in fully.

Once the cake is cooled, you're ready to layer it up. Put the first layer flat side down on a serving plate. Spoon one-third of the frosting on top, smooth it around, then add the next layer of cake. Continue this until you have frosted the top of the cake, decorate with the walnuts and mint leaves, then serve.

Tricks of the Trade

Jam sugar is sometimes also known as gelling sugar or jelly sugar. If you can't find it, you can use regular sugar and pectin, but you will need to follow the instructions on the pectin package, as they can vary.

Homemade jams will keep longer when stored in clean, sterilized jars. To do this, wash them really well in soapy water, then submerge them in water in a large pot and boil vigorously for 10 minutes. (If you live at an altitude higher than 1,000 feet/ 305 meters, add one additional minute for each additional 1,000 feet/305 meters of elevation.)

White chocolate is the secret ingredient here, because it will make your fudge taste professional: it gives it a really good consistency, that smoothness which means you will see your teeth marks when you bite into it (though, if you like crumbly fudge, this isn't the recipe for you). I use superfine rather than granulated sugar, as it's less likely to crystallize.

You will need a kitchen thermometer; don't try to start freestyling this recipe. Make sure your thermometer works by putting it in a pot of boiling water and checking it measures 212°F (100°C).

It's important to use Irish or at least British butter here, because of their low whey and high fat contents.

IRISH BUTTERED FUDGE WITH A SECRET INGREDIENT

1½ cups (315 g) superfine sugar
1⅓ cups (315 ml) heavy cream
scant ½ cup (100 ml) liquid glucose
3½ tablespoons salted Irish butter, chopped, plus more for the pan
3½ oz (100 g) white chocolate, finely chopped

Put the sugar, cream and glucose in a large saucepan, set it over medium heat and keep an eye on it, giving it a whisk occasionally. Butter a square 10 in x 2½ in (25 × 1 cm) dish or plastic container and line it with parchment paper.

Bring the sugar mixture up to 250°F (121°C). Once it reaches around 240°F (115°C) it will be prone to burning on the bottom, so make sure you stir it constantly. If you are unlucky and it burns, switch pots immediately.

Once the mixture reaches temperature, it will be light brown in color and you will have noticed the quality of its bubbles becoming larger and more viscous. Take it off the heat.

Quickly beat in half the chocolate, then half the butter, mixing to combine them with a whisk, then repeat to add the remaining chocolate and butter. When it is all combined, pour into the prepared dish or container and leave to set until cooled.

Place in the fridge to chill overnight.

Turn out onto a chopping board and cut into fudge squares. Store in an airtight box, with the layers of pieces stacked in between sheets of parchment paper. The fudge will last for weeks in the fridge, or a couple of months in the freezer.

Sweets

I have to confess I don't have a particularly sweet tooth, but I am human, so I love a soft moist cake with whipped unsweetened cream and fruit. Who doesn't?

Due to the fact—I can only assume—that I was born with ovaries, I was put in the pastry section when I started work in professional kitchens, whether I liked it or not. And it turned out that, although I may not always order a dessert, I certainly love learning how to make them. I love the detail and how—if rules aren't followed—things can go drastically wrong. I eventually escaped from the pastry section after three or four years, but it was a privilege to have been trained by the wonderful chef Mary (Knox) McEvoy. She taught me everything I know about desserts and that knowledge has stood me well over the years. Mary didn't just teach me about pastry though; she encouraged me to help others when asked and to do a task quickly during a restaurant service, because, if you don't start with speed, you'll end up overwhelmed in the middle of dinner.

The dessert recipes I have included in this chapter are focused on sharing with others. Some of the dishes are easy, such as the lemongrass posset, while others take a bit of time, such as the large cakes. But there's a reason for them all: sometimes making a large cake for a crowd is easier and more affordable than creating three of a more regular size, for instance.

I have chosen recipes here to appeal both to people who love sweet things and to those who don't think they do. You never know, I may just persuade you...

This is an important recipe for me. A staple for Celts and part of our heritage, these are something everyone should be able to cook. And I am very happy to say I love them, as oat cookies of any sort are my go-to. These are on the sweeter side of the oat cake spectrum, so you can have them on the side of a dessert, as well as with your cheese, or just as a snack. However, the recipe is lovely sweet or savory; just reduce the sugar by half for a more savory oat cake. And usefully, you should be able to replace the flour here with a gluten-free alternative, gram for gram, and get an excellent result.

Don't be afraid to get right in when mixing this recipe, using your hands. The more you mix all the ingredients together, the better these oat cakes will be.

OAT CAKES

MAKES ABOUT 30

1 stick (125 g) unsalted butter
2½ cups (225 g) old fashioned oats
scant 1 cup (110 g) all-purpose flour
¾ cup (140 g) sugar
1 teaspoon baking powder
pinch of fine sea salt
1 teaspoon ground ginger
seeds from 7 cardamom pods, or ½ teaspoon ground cardamom seeds
1–2 tablespoons water

Melt the butter in a pan and leave it to cool down.

Preheat the oven to 350°F (180°C). Line a couple of baking sheets with parchment paper.

Put all the dry ingredients in a mixing bowl. Sprinkle in the slightly cooled melted butter and rub it in with your fingers until it's evenly mixed through, then make a well in the center. Now add 1 tablespoon of the water to the well and really massage the contents of the bowl, combining the ingredients and making sure to work the mixture a lot with your hands to slightly break down the oats. If it's too dry, add a touch more water to the mix and continue to massage. When the mixture sticks together, it's ready.

Once it's all mixed, roll out the dough between 2 sheets of parchment paper until it's about ⅛ in (3 mm) thick.

Remove the top layer of parchment paper and cut out circles, or whatever other shapes you prefer for your oat cakes, with cookie cutters, then move them to the prepared baking sheets.

Bake for 10–15 minutes, or until golden brown in color. Store in an airtight container, where they will keep for 2 weeks. If they get soft, throw them back in the oven briefly to crisp up.

My dad grew up in Ringsend, by the sea in Dublin. When he was young, a ship came into the dock carrying a load of bananas. The cargo was left unsupervised, so he took a stick of bananas— it seems bonkers to me now—and ran home with them on his shoulder. Back then, bananas would have been a super-luxury. Even though he knew they weren't ripe, he recruited his younger brother—my uncle Tony—to help him eat some. They filled their bellies with the green bananas and, when my grandmother came home, she found two of her sons on the floor holding their bellies and crying. She was so worried! Well, at least until my (devout Catholic) grandmother found out they had gorged on stolen bananas... I'm pretty sure the boys were given a piece of her mind.

Though we photographed the recipe here with a halved banana on top, be aware that—should you want to do the same—it adds jeopardy to the bread, as it may not cook through correctly. I've left it off in the recipe and suggest you do the same.

Traditionally, throughout Ireland, caraway was used in sweet recipes and I use it a lot at home and in my restaurant. It's a great flavor that can spice a recipe up without any heat. Now DO NOT throw your banana skins away. If you are looking for a recipe that will blow your mind, turn to page 90 for my vegan pulled pork made with banana skins. Yes, really.

SPICED BANANA BREAD

MAKES 1 LOAF

1 stick (120 g) unsalted butter, at room temperature, plus more for the pan
½ cup (120 g) brown sugar, or ½ cup (110 g) white sugar plus 1 tablespoon black treacle or molasses
2 teaspoons ground cinnamon
1 tablespoon caraway seeds
3 ripe or over-ripe bananas, mashed with a fork
2 eggs, at room temperature
1 cup (120 g) self-rising flour
1 tablespoon milk, if needed
fine sea salt

Preheat the oven to 350°F (180°C). Butter an 8½ in x 4½ in (1 lb/500 g) loaf pan.

In a stand mixer fitted with the paddle attachment, or using an electric hand mixer and a bowl, cream your butter, sugar, treacle or molasses (if using), cinnamon and caraway on a medium speed. Beat for 5 minutes, until lighter in color and creamy in texture.

Add your mashed bananas, a pinch of salt, 1 egg and half the flour. Mix well. Add your second egg and mix well again. Now add the last of your flour, with the milk, if needed, to give a dropping consistency. Scrape the batter into the prepared pan.

Bake for 55–65 minutes. Use a metal skewer to dip into the center of the cake and, if it comes out clean, the loaf is baked. If there is any batter on the skewer, put the pan back into the oven for 5 minutes to finish cooking.

I like to toast slices of this and spread them with salted butter.

We grew up with home-baked scones as a very regular treat. Cakes and sweet things bought in the shops were strictly for Saturdays. My mother only made scones in a triangle shape, which is a genius way to get the maximum portions from your dough, plus if you don't have cutters, well, it's a win-win.

If you don't have buttermilk or yogurt for the scones, you can substitute around ½ cup (100–120 ml) whole milk instead.

My mother's jam recipe is simple, but don't you think that means it won't be special. I dream of gooseberry jam all year round, so, if you are lucky to grow gooseberries out in your garden, then harvest those valuable jewels and make this!

THE PERFECT FLUFFY SCONES, WITH HOMEMADE GOOSEBERRY JAM

Preheat the oven to 375°F (190°C). Line a baking sheet with parchment paper.

For the scones, mix all the dry ingredients together. Grate the extremely cold butter straight into your dry ingredients, then crumble the mixture between your fingertips, rubbing it together and lifting high in the air. A quick game is a good game, so you don't warm the butter.

Mix the liquid ingredients in a jug. Create a well in the center of the flour and add your liquids. Stir from the center, moving outwards with the spoon. When the flour is almost mixed in, you'll need to get your hands in and give it a very quick knead: less is more for a soft, fluffy texture.

You can, of course, make this in a stand mixer. Use the same process and doubly make sure you do not overwork it.

Dust a work surface with flour and roll the dough out to 1 in (3 cm) thick, then shape it with your hands into a rough square. Cut into 3 strips with a sharp knife, then cut each of those into as close to triangles as you can. If they are a little misshapen, it's all good. Try to cut them all out now, though you can reroll the mix once more and cut into triangles again. (If you use a cutter instead and have any dough left over, you can make it into rock bun bites, by adding raisins and rolling in sugar.)

FOR THE SCONES

3 cups (350 g) self-rising flour,
 plus more to dust
1 teaspoon baking powder
⅓ cup (40 g) confectioners' sugar
6 tablespoons (85 g) unsalted
 butter, very cold from the fridge,
 or frozen
scant 1 cup (200 g) buttermilk,
 or plain yogurt (or see recipe
 introduction)
1 egg, lightly beaten
1 teaspoon vanilla extract

FOR THE JAM

2 lb 3 oz (1 kg) gooseberries
4½ cups (900 g) jam sugar
 (see page 213)
scant ½ cup (100 ml) water

Place the scones on a baking sheet lined with parchment paper and bake in the oven for 15 minutes.

Leave to cool, but these are best eaten as soon as possible, even with a breath of the oven still about them, with salted butter, jam and unsweetened whipped or clotted cream.

Wash and top and tail (trim) the gooseberries. This takes a bit of time, so do it while you watch TV or listen to a podcast. Put a saucer in the fridge or freezer.

Put the sugar in a heavy-based pot with the measured water. Place over medium-low heat and heat slowly, stirring occasionally, until the sugar has completely dissolved. You do not want the sugar to change color. Add the gooseberries and cook for 20 minutes.

To test the set, you have 2 options. Check on a kitchen thermometer: it is ready when it has reached 220°F (105°C). Or take a small amount of jam and put it on the chilled saucer. (Turn off the heat while testing, to avoid overcooking.) Leave for 5 minutes. Run your finger through the jam: it should hold a strong line where your finger was. If it runs back together, keep cooking for another 10–15 minutes. Whichever test you are using, perform it again and again until the jam is ready to take off the heat.

Put the still-hot jam into still-hot sterilized jars (see page 213), leaving ¼ in (.66 cm) space at the top. You can process the jam (for 10 minutes) in a water bath canner for longer term storage, or store in the fridge or freezer.

Tricks of the Trade

If you only have a small amount of gooseberries, make use of their high pectin content by mixing them with blackcurrants, or even apples, in other jams and jellies, to help those to set.

This cake is crazy-easy and stays fresh in the fridge for three days. Though it has a high sugar content, the bitter Guinness and sour buttermilk provide balance and, together, they are why the cake stays fresh for so long. It's a great birthday cake—the one I make most for people—that you can make well in advance, as both the cake and the cream freeze very well. Even my son has been fed it, as the alcohol is cooked off. This is a very wet batter, so don't worry: that's the way it's supposed to be.

GUINNESS CHOCOLATE CAKE

FOR THE SPONGE
2 cups (500 ml) Guinness
1 stick (125 g) unsalted butter,
    plus more for the pans
generous 1 cup (140 g) all-
    purpose flour
1 cup (200 g) sugar
scant ½ cup (35 g) cocoa powder
1 teaspoon baking soda
½ teaspoon baking powder
pinch of fine sea salt
1 egg, lightly beaten
⅓ cup (75 ml) buttermilk

FOR THE CREAM
1¼ cups (300 ml) heavy cream
½ cup (60 g) confectioners' sugar
3½ tablespoons buttermilk
2 tablespoons mascarpone
1 vanilla bean, seeds scraped out

Place a saucepan under an extraction fan, pour in the Guinness and set over high heat. Reduce to half the quantity (1 cup/ 250 ml). Set aside to cool. Melt the butter in a separate pan, then leave it to cool.

Butter 2 jelly roll pans, each about 12 x 8 in (30 × 20 cm), and line with parchment paper. Preheat the oven to 350°F (180°C).

Place the flour, sugar, cocoa, baking soda, baking powder and salt in a bowl, whisk to mix, then make a well in the center. Add ½ cup (125 ml) of the Guinness reduction with the cooled melted butter, egg and buttermilk and whisk the batter until no lumps are left.

Divide the mixture between the 2 prepared pans, then bake for 10 minutes. Insert a metal skewer into the center: when it emerges, it should be clean; also the cake should bounce back to the touch. It should be just cooked, rather than overcooked. The mix is wet and you really need to use a metal skewer to check it's done in the center. Leave in the pans to cool, then put a rack over the pans and turn them out. Leave until cold, then chill. The cake needs to be chilled when you're cutting it to assemble the cake. Halve both chilled cakes widthways, then trim the cakes so you have 4 matching flat layers that will sit neatly on top of each other.

Whip together the cream, confectioners' sugar, buttermilk, mascarpone and vanilla seeds to soft peaks (see below). Use this to sandwich the cake layers together. Serve in slices, so you see the layers.

Tricks of the Trade

Adding mascarpone to heavy cream is an amazing tip given to me by a fantastic pastry chef, Rey (Hortillosa) Encarnacion from the Conrad Hotel in Dublin. When you add mascarpone to whipped cream, it never loses its air and is less likely to split.

This is my idea of a perfect dessert, something I often cook for a dinner party, because I like to eat it (and I am fussy about desserts). It's not only bursting with flavor, but it's very convenient to make and serve. It's zingy, sweet and sharp all at the same time: just what you want after a big meal.

Recipes don't get much easier than this. At the end, you have a luscious pudding that your friends and family will rave about. You can serve it with shortbread cookies on the side, or lovely sweet Oat cakes (see page 220).

We don't use mint enough in desserts, in my opinion. It's probably because we chefs overdid it with the leaves twenty years ago! I use it a lot; I find it pairs brilliantly with so many other flavors.

LEMON, LEMONGRASS & CARDAMOM POSSET

MAKES 6

FOR THE LEMON REDUCTION
juice of 2 lemons (see below)
seeds of 4 green cardamom
 pods, crushed

FOR THE POSSET
1 cup (200 g) sugar
2 cups (500 ml) heavy cream
2 lemongrass stalks, trimmed

TO SERVE
finely grated lemon zest
small mint leaves
Oat cakes (see page 220),
 or shortbread cookies

First make the reduction: put the lemon juice in a saucepan and reduce by half. Once done, add the ground cardamom seeds, return to a boil, then leave to cool.

Add all the other ingredients for the posset to the pan, bruising the lemongrass stalks with the back of a heavy knife or a rolling pin to release their aroma, then bring to a boil.

Pass through a sieve, then pour into 6 glasses. Do not move the glasses for 10 minutes: this will allow the posset to set slightly, so when you do move them to the fridge, the mix doesn't splash up the sides of the glasses.

Leave for as long as you can in the fridge, ideally overnight. Serve with lemon zest and ripped mint leaves on top and cookies on the side.

Tricks of the Trade

Don't waste the zest of lemons when you only need their juice for a recipe. Instead, infuse the zest in a bottle of olive oil, or put it in a container of granulated sugar. This citrus-scented sugar is a secret weapon which will gently flavor cakes and other bakes. Or, of course, just freeze the zest as it is for another time.

Yes, this is dessert, but as the recipe uses buttermilk, it's practically a health food! Just like real yogurt, we take buttermilk for granted, but it contains live cultures that are supposed to be included in everyone's daily diet. They are excellent for the health of your gut.

Panna cotta is a staple dessert for me, both at home and in the restaurant. It's simple and elegant and very easy to scale up to feed a crowd. I never tire of it. As the end of a meal, it works year round, because of the infinite ways in which you can change what you serve alongside it. This version is for midsummer, but it sits well alongside pink rhubarb in deep winter, too, or mangos in springtime, just as they arrive in season from India.

To add a little texture, serve a cookie or shortbread alongside, or consider making a sweet crumble, baked in the oven to add crispness, to strew over the top.

BUTTERMILK PANNA COTTA WITH LIGHTLY POACHED STRAWBERRIES & RIPPED BASIL

Put the gelatin powder in a small bowl with 1 tablespoon cold water and leave it to "bloom" (dissolve and hydrate) while you prepare the cream mixture.

With a sharp knife, split the vanilla bean lengthways, then use the tip of the knife to scrape the seeds out into a saucepan. Add the cream to the pan with the pod. (This will add extra flavor and you will be straining the mixture later.) Add the sugar and place the saucepan over medium-high heat, stirring occasionally, until you are sure that the sugar has all dissolved.

Once the cream is steaming—just before it boils—remove it from the heat and add the hydrated gelatin to the hot mixture, stirring to dissolve it. Next add the lemon juice, tasting the mixture to make sure it's acidic enough and adding more juice if you think it needs it (but remember you will be adding the tart buttermilk in a little while). Pass the mixture through a sieve into a heatproof bowl, then set this bowl into an ice bath (a larger bowl filled with ice cubes), stirring as it gradually cools.

FOR THE PANNA COTTA

1 teaspoon unflavored gelatine
   powder
1 vanilla bean
1¼ cups (300 ml) heavy cream
⅓ cup (75 g) sugar
juice of 1 lemon, plus more
   if needed
1¼ cups (300 ml) buttermilk
leaves from ½ bunch of basil,
   to serve

FOR THE STRAWBERRIES

¼ cup (50 g) sugar
finely grated zest and juice
   of 1 lime
1 lb 2 oz (500 g) strawberries,
   hulled and halved

It's a good idea to dry the vanilla bean on a sheet of paper towels, then seal it in a jar of sugar, to give you vanilla sugar. (You can add more spent vanilla beans and sugar to the jar as you use them.)

Once the cream mixture is cool, mix it with the buttermilk and pour into 4–6 wine glasses. Place in the fridge to set for at least 4 hours, but preferably overnight.

Meanwhile, get on with the strawberries. Place the sugar in a saucepan with the lime juice and strawberries and cook over medium heat, covered with the lid, for about 5 minutes, stirring occasionally. Let cool. When the berries are cool, add the lime zest.

Top the panna cottas with the lightly poached strawberries and ripped basil leaves.

Part of the reason I love caraway is that it's a flavor that is equally at home with both sweet and savory foods. You can stick the seeds in coleslaw, or scatter them over chicken breasts before roasting, as a great "extra" flavor. Chefs forget to tell the home cook that the layering of flavors—such as veggies, spices and nuts—gives real length of flavor and complexity to a dish. As you taste this, you will experience more layers of flavor coming in.

CHOCOLATE & CARAWAY MOUSSE

SERVES 6-8

10½ oz (300 g) dark chocolate, minimum 56% cocoa solids, broken into small pieces
7 large egg yolks
¾ cup (140 g) superfine sugar
1 teaspoon ground caraway seeds
1¾ cups (400 ml) heavy cream
fine sea salt

Put the chocolate into a large heatproof bowl and set that over a pan of simmering water (make sure the bowl does not touch the water). Melt the chocolate, then leave to cool slightly.

Whisk the egg yolks with the sugar and caraway seeds until pale and thick.

Separately whip the cream to soft peaks, then fold this into the egg yolk mixture.

Fold the melted chocolate into the cream mixture, along with a pinch of salt. Divide among glasses and chill.

When I was a child, every birthday party had a chocolate cookie cake, and I loved it. When I became an adult, I realized I could put whatever I wanted in such a cake and that it wasn't compulsory to stick to digestive cookies! So I took a trip to the shops, went a bit wild and bought loads of chocolate bars. I experimented with many different combinations—all in the name of science, of course—came to this version and thought it was the most fun. As well as tasting great, it looks quite dramatic and beautiful.

This remains really good to serve at a special occasion to guests of any age—I find it's always the first thing to disappear and the adults are usually to blame—and it's also excellent to keep chilled for an after-dinner treat at the end of a long day. It stays good in the fridge for a very long time. And, of course, kids love it.

VA-VA-VOOM CHOCOLATE COOKIE CAKE

SERVES 8 GENEROUSLY

10½ oz (300 g) dark chocolate, minimum 56% cocoa solids, chopped into small pieces
10½ oz (300 g) milk chocolate, chopped into small pieces
3½ oz (100 g) unsalted butter, chopped
scant ½ cup (100 ml) heavy cream
2 chocolate bars with nougat, such as Double Decker, Milky Way, or Snickers
2 × 2-bar caramel-shortbread chocolate bars, such as Twix
2 chocolate honeycomb bars, such as Crunchies
6 shortbread cookie fingers

Line a 9½ x 5 in (2 lb/900 g) loaf pan with plastic wrap, parchment paper or reusable nonstick baking liner.

Place the dark and milk chocolates and the butter in a heatproof bowl. Place the bowl over a saucepan of gently simmering water, making sure the bowl does not touch the water. Stir occasionally until melted, then remove the bowl from the heat, pour in the cream and mix well.

Pour one-third of the melted chocolate mixture into the prepared pan and layer the chocolate bars with nougat and caramel-shortbread chocolate bars over it.

Now pour on another one-third of the chocolate and cream mixture. Add the chocolate honeycomb bars (you may not fit them all in: cook's treat), and shortbread fingers on top. Pour the remaining melted chocolate over the top of that.

Place in the fridge for a good couple of hours until completely set, though ideally leaving it overnight would be good. Cut into slices—a knife dipped into boiling water and wiped dry between cuts helps to create neat slices—and serve.

If you or any of your guests are gluten-free, the tart filling recipe here can be made in individual glasses or ramekins and served as a chocolate pot.

You can swap out the lime for any other citrus you prefer, as the chocolate tart will love them all. I think it's particularly brilliant with grapefruit zest, and with grapefruit segments served alongside.

During the winter, citrus are at their very best and their oils will give you much more flavor. At other times of year, the flavor will be more muted, so taste your chocolate mixture to check you have the level of zest you want. If not, add a bit more.

DOUBLE CHOCOLATE & LIME TART

Place the flour and butter in the bowl of an electric mixer fitted with the paddle attachment, or in a food processor. Mix until you have fine crumbs, then stir in the sugar. Add the measured water gradually until it becomes a dough (you may need to add more water, if it seems dry). Wrap in plastic or reusable wrap and put in the fridge to rest for 30 minutes, or up to 2 days.

Preheat the oven to 375°F (190°C). Find a 9 in (23 cm) cake pan, or tart pan with removable base, and butter it well.

Roll the pastry out on a work surface dusted with flour until ⅛ in (3 mm) thick. Line the cake pan or tart pan with the pastry and trim it neatly. Scrunch up a piece of parchment paper large enough to cover the whole of the pastry shell, then unscrunch it and use it to line the pastry. Fill it with dried lentils, or dried beans, or raw rice, or pie weights, until their level reaches the top of the pastry shell, being sure to get none of them directly on the pastry (or they will bake into the pastry).

Bake the pastry shell for 10 minutes until the edges start to turn golden brown, then remove the lentils or beans or rice or pie weights and the parchment paper and cook the pastry for a further 10–15 minutes or until the base starts to turn golden brown and is fully cooked through. This is called baking blind, a process in which the dried beans, rice

FOR THE SWEET PASTRY

2 cups (250 g) all-purpose flour,
plus more to dust
1 stick (125 g) unsalted butter,
chilled and chopped, plus more
for the pan
⅓ cup (65 g) sugar
2 tablespoons water, plus more
if needed

FOR THE CHOCOLATE FILLING

7 oz (200 g) chocolate, at least
38% cocoa solids, broken
into pieces
7 oz (200 g) white chocolate,
broken into pieces
generous 1 cup (280 g)
heavy cream
3½ tablespoons unsalted butter,
at room temperature, chopped
2 limes, plus more lime zest
(optional) if needed and
to serve
cocoa powder, to dust
crème fraîche, to serve

or pie weights absorb the heat of the oven to cook the pastry shell, without it rising or burning.

Set the pastry aside to cool. While it is cooling, you can make the filling.

Put both types of chopped chocolate into a heatproof bowl. Bring your cream up to a boil in a saucepan, then pour it over your chocolate. Let it sit for 2 minutes, then whisk by hand until smooth. Whisk in the soft butter, then finely zest your 2 limes directly into the mixture. Stir well. Taste the mixture to see if the lime flavor is at the right level for you, adding more zest if you would like it stronger (see recipe introduction). Pour into your cooled tart shell. Place in the fridge for 1 hour to set.

When ready to serve, dust with cocoa powder and some more lime zest, if you like. Serve with a spoon of crème fraîche.

Tricks of the Trade

Any sweet pastry that you have left over can be rolled out on a lightly floured surface, cut into circles, glazed with beaten egg or milk, sprinkled with sugar and cinnamon, then arranged on a baking pan and baked as cookies for 10–15 minutes, or until golden. Leave to cool on the baking pan, so they crisp up, before you try to move them.

This dessert means a lot to me as I learned how to make sabayon as a first-year apprentice at Cathal Brugha Street DIT in Dublin.

Desserts like this do not come around too often. Although it is a very simple recipe, it's incredibly elegant. Berries work really well as a summer variation and are easier to prepare.

CITRUS SABAYON

SERVES 2

2 medium oranges
1 ruby grapefruit
4 teaspoons Cointreau
3 large egg yolks
2 tablespoons sugar

Finely grate the zest from 1 orange, then slice the tops and bottoms from both the oranges and the grapefruit.

Sitting one of the fruits on its base, with a sharp knife remove all the skin and pith (the white stuff), curving the knife down the sides as though it were a barrel. Working over a bowl, slice the knife between the membranes on either side of each segment so it falls into the bowl, along with any juice. Repeat to peel and segment all the citrus fruits.

Add the Cointreau to the bowl, stir gently, then set aside and allow to marinate for 10 minutes.

Place a heatproof bowl over a saucepan half-filled with just-boiled water and place over low heat. Do not allow the water to touch the bowl.

Strain the citrus segments through a sieve over a bowl. Add the egg yolks to the bowl with the sugar and orange zest and set it over the saucepan of simmering water.

Whisk with a balloon whisk for 8–10 minutes, or until the mixture is very light, pale and thick. The whisk should leave a ribbon trail when lifted: you should be able to write the number "8" on the surface.

Arrange the orange and ruby grapefruit segments in a shallow flameproof dish or plate.

Carefully remove the bowl of sabayon from the hot water and spoon the mixture over the citrus segments. Place close to a very hot broiler, watching closely, or gently brûlée with a chef's blowtorch, until lightly browned in places. Serve warm.

One of the reasons why I put this cake in the book was that, when I was a child, I believed there was some sort of magical whimsy attached to Black Forest gateau. My mother never ever made chocolate cake, but, when we went to a restaurant, we would see the dessert trolleys roll past laden with a whole panoply of temptations... along with their version of Black Forest gateau. I knew what it was, of course, but there is something about Black Forest gateau in particular that is so uncannily good.

It's the kirsch syrup on the cake—the magic of the soak—adding both moisture and a flavor you can't quite put your finger on. It makes this cake better than any regular chocolate-cake-with-chocolate-frosting affair. I'm not keen on cakes unless they are soaked in syrup; then I'm obsessed with them.

One taste of this and I'm transported back in time to those dessert trolley days. If the assembly sounds too much, don't be afraid to serve slices of the cake with the cherries in syrup spooned on top and a bowl of the cream on the side. A marvelous dessert.

If you don't have kirsch in the pantry at home, Cointreau or even Kahlua are nice alternatives.

BLACK FOREST GATEAU

If you can, cook the cherries the day before you make the cake, so they can infuse with the star anise overnight. Pit them first; I find it easiest to halve fresh cherries, then quarter the half with the pit and twist, in order to remove it. You can of course use a cherry pitter, if you have one.

Put the cherries, sugar and star anise in a wide-based pan with the measured water (if the cherries are frozen, make sure they are defrosted first). Set over medium heat and cook for about 5 minutes, stirring occasionally, until the cherries are almost softened and releasing their juice. Taste and adjust the sugar, if needed. Cover and allow to cool, add the kirsch, then refrigerate. Leave it overnight, if you have time, to allow the flavor of the star anise to come through; the syrup needs to be chilled before you use it.

Preheat the oven to 375°F (190°C). Butter 2 × 8 in (20 cm) cake pans and line with parchment paper.

Melt the butter, then leave it to cool slightly.

FOR THE CHERRIES

14 oz (400 g) fresh black cherries,
   or 10½ oz (300 g) frozen and
   defrosted black cherries
¼ cup (50 g) sugar, or to taste
3 star anise
1 tablespoon water
3½ tablespoons kirsch

FOR THE SPONGE CAKE

13 tablespoons (200 g) unsalted
   butter, plus more for the pans
1⅔ cups (200 g) self-rising flour
½ cup (50 g) cocoa powder, sifted
1 cup (200 g) sugar
pinch of salt
2 medium eggs, lightly beaten
up to 3½ tablespoons milk,
   if needed

FOR THE CREAM

scant 1 cup (200 ml) heavy cream
2 tablespoons mascarpone
grated dark chocolate, to
   serve (optional)

Mix the flour and cocoa powder together in a bowl with the sugar and salt. Make a well in the center.

Pour the slightly cooled melted butter into the well with the eggs and mix until you have a thick batter. You may need to add the milk, a little at a time, if it looks a bit dry.

Split the batter between the prepared pans. Bake for 20 minutes, or until the cakes are risen and bouncy to the touch. Leave to cool for 10–15 minutes, then turn out and transfer to a board, still on the parchment paper, until completely cooled. Chill until ready to assemble.

As a rule, I always prefer whipped cream unsweetened, as there's already enough sugar in desserts and a cool creamy contrast is very effective. Whip together the cream and mascarpone to soft peaks; as always, be careful not to overwhip. Again, chill the cream.

When you are ready to build the cake, everything—cherries, cake and cream—needs to be chilled. Drain the cherries in a sieve over a bowl, reserving the syrup (discard the star anise).

Once the cakes are chilled, carefully peel off the parchment paper. Brush the cherry syrup over both cake layers. This gives extra depth of flavor and helps keep the cake fresher, though it's so delicious it's likely to be eaten up lickedy-quick.

Now select your base cake layer, put it on a serving plate and spoon the cream on top, then spoon over some cherries, allowing the syrup to run down the sides. Place the second cake on top.

Pile on the remaining cream, followed by the rest of the cherries. Grate over some chocolate, if you like, then serve.

This is an adaptation of a technical French dessert called a crémeux, but do not let that put you off! I was frightened of it at first, but once I finally approached it, I realized how easy it was. All you need to do is give it a bit of time in the fridge.

I keep the flavors simple here, but you can jazz this up with all sorts of treats, such as infusing the hot cream with edible lavender, or a bit of chile (sounds crazy, is delicious). Leave it to infuse for 30 minutes or so before very gently reheating (don't let it boil), then straining and adding to the white chocolate.

This is great with poached plums alongside.

WHIPPED WHITE CHOCOLATE DREAM

SERVES 4

6 oz (170 g) white chocolate,
    finely chopped
1¼ cups (300 ml) heavy cream
1 vanilla bean, split lengthways
    and seeds scraped out
finely grated orange zest, to serve
chopped pistachio nuts, to
    serve (optional)

Put the chocolate into a large heatproof bowl. Bring a scant 1 cup (200 ml) of the cream to a boil with the vanilla seeds and pod. Pour the hot cream over the chocolate and leave for 3 minutes. Stir until smooth, then cover and set the bowl in the fridge until chilled.

Once the chocolate mixture is set and chilled, remove the vanilla bean and pour in the remaining cream. Whip the mixture until it is light and airy.

Leave to set in the fridge for 24 hours, then sprinkle with the orange zest and chopped pistachios, if using, and serve with your favorite cookies.

Tricks of the Trade

For a fancy presentation, chill the mixture in a container. Put a serving spoon into a cup of just-boiled water. When the spoon is hot, use it to scoop the mixture and drop it in curls onto serving dishes, before scattering with the orange zest and pistachios.

Mammy only ever used a pie plate to make an apple tart. As I'm typing this, my memory is taking me back in time to when I was a little kid; my mother's kitchen helper. She's holding the plate and quick-cutting the overhanging pastry off the sides, I'm catching the pastry scraps and am proudly in charge of transforming them into decorations for the top. I was very fond of covering the tart with pastry leaves. It's her pie plate that you see in the photograph here. As a child, I loved sugar, but my mother never added sugar to whipped cream. Back then, I thought that was because she didn't want us to have too much sugar, but now as an adult I realize the cool relief that unsweetened cream gives a dessert.

Bramley apples, when cooked, break down very quickly. If you do not have access to Bramleys, I recommend chopping your apples very finely and cooking them into a compote first, before chilling and placing in the pastry base. You may have more pastry than you need. If you do, just make it into lovely cookies (see page 241).

MAMMY'S APPLE TART ON A PLATE

FOR THE PASTRY
1¾ cups (225 g) all-purpose flour, plus more to dust
pinch of fine sea salt
2½ tablespoons sugar
10 tablespoons (150 g) unsalted butter, very cold from the fridge, or frozen, plus more for the pan
3 tablespoons water

FOR THE FILLING
1 lb 9 oz (700 g) cooking apples, peeled and chopped
⅓ cup (80 g) sugar, plus more if needed (if the apples are extra tart)
½ teaspoon ground cloves, or 1 teaspoon ground cinnamon
1 egg, lightly beaten

scant 1 cup (200 ml) heavy cream, softly whipped, to serve

Put your flour, salt and sugar in a bowl, grate in the very cold butter and, using the tips of your fingers, rub the butter into the flour mixture until it looks like crumbs. Add the measured water and work it quickly into a dough. Wrap the ball of dough and let it rest in the fridge for 1 hour.

Preheat the oven to 410°F (210°C).

Rub your pie plate (or pan) with butter and dust with flour: this will prevent the pastry from sticking to the plate.

Dust a work surface with flour. Cut your pastry in half and roll one piece out into a circle that will fill the prepared pan, then use it to line the pan. Tip your chopped apples into the pastry-lined pan and sprinkle with the sugar and spice.

Roll out the other half of the pastry, wetting the outside rim with a little water so the pastry top sticks to the bottom, and drape it over the filling, pressing the rim to seal. Cut around the pan to remove the overhanging dough and use these scraps to create a decoration. Brush the pie and decorations with the beaten egg and bake for 30 minutes. Make sure the pastry is golden brown before you remove it from the oven, otherwise the pastry on the bottom won't be cooked.

Serve with the whipped cream.

As a kid we didn't get desserts every day, only on Sundays. It was often stewed apple and custard, or Mammy's apple tart (see page 253), but every now and again we would be treated to rhubarb and custard... and I would be giddy with delight. This is the closest you'll get to a rhubarb trifle without the hassle. It's delicious hot or cold.

You'll know how you prefer your custard, so though the recipe below is how I want it—in thick dollops—adjusting the level of cornstarch gives drastically different results (see below). Oh, and the juices from the rhubarb make a delicious syrup you can dilute with water or seltzer for a refreshing drink.

RHUBARB & CUSTARD WITH SHERRIED ALMONDS

SERVES 4

FOR THE RHUBARB
1 lb 2 oz (500 g) forced pink
   rhubarb
1 cup (200 g) sugar
scant ½ cup (100 ml) water

FOR THE CUSTARD
scant 1 cup (200 ml) whole milk
2½ cups (600 ml) heavy cream
1 vanilla bean, halved lengthways
   and seeds scraped out
½ cup (100 g) sugar, or to taste
3 eggs
3 tablespoons cornstarch

TO SERVE
4 tablespoons sliced almonds
1–2 tablespoons confectioners'
   sugar
splash of sherry

Preheat the oven to 250°F (120°C): low and slow will protect the color of the forced rhubarb. Trim your rhubarb into ¾ in (2 cm) pieces and place in an ovenproof dish with the sugar and measured water. Cover with foil and cook for 20 minutes. It is ready when you can push the flesh and it gives way. Let the rhubarb rest in its juices while you make the custard.

Put the milk, cream, scraped-out vanilla seeds and empty vanilla pod in a saucepan and bring slowly to a boil.

Whisk the sugar, eggs and cornstarch together in a heatproof bowl and slowly pour the boiled cream on top, while whisking to stop the eggs from scrambling. Strain back into the pan, set over a low heat and, stirring continually, bring to a boil. Taste for sweetness and add sugar if you like.

Toast the almonds in a dry frying pan. When they start to turn brown, sift over the confectioners' sugar and stir to caramelize, then splash in the sherry and stir until it evaporates. Tip onto a sheet of parchment paper and set aside to cool.

Strain the juice from the rhubarb (reserve it; see recipe introduction). Spoon the rhubarb into dishes, along with the custard and sherried almonds.

Tricks of the Trade

To adjust the thickness of custard:
- No cornstarch at all gives a silky, pouring custard.
- 1 tablespoon cornstarch creates a thick pouring custard.
- 2 tablespoons cornstarch results in a thick custard.
- 3 tablespoons cornstarch makes a custard that sits in thick dollops, even when it's hot.

If you ever get the urge for something sweet, but don't feel like preheating your oven and spending an hour making a cake, this recipe is great, as you can create it from start to finish in just ten minutes. If you are going to devour the cake while warm, I would say you could leave out the oil, though it is needed if you will be eating it the next day.

"Mug cakes" have become wildly popular recently, but the cakes can seize up and become tough, mainly because of their depth. Cooking microwave cake in a shallow dish removes that risk.

CHOCOLATE-BEET MICROWAVE SHEET CAKE

SERVES 4

FOR THE CAKE
1 egg, lightly beaten
1½ tablespoons vegetable oil
1 tablespoon water
1 tablespoon milk
1 small raw beet, grated (though if you only have cooked beet it will still work, as long as it is not in vinegar!), about 3½ oz (100 g) total weight
½ cup (60 g) self-rising flour
¼ cup (20 g) cocoa powder
⅓ cup (70 g) sugar

TO SERVE
scant ½ cup (100 ml) heavy cream
1¾ oz (50 g) dark chocolate, about 56% cocoa solids, chopped
edible rose petals (optional)

Mix all the wet ingredients for the cake together in a bowl with the grated beet. In a separate bowl, mix all the dry ingredients together and create a well in the center. Pour the liquids into the well and whisk until you have a smooth batter.

Pour into a microwave-safe dish or a silicone mold, in which the batter will lie no more than about 1 in (2.5 cm) deep. Cook in a 650-watt microwave on medium heat for 3 minutes, then on high for 2 minutes. It may not look completely baked, but with microwave cooking you really need to bear the concept of residual heat cooking (see page 113) at the front of your mind. Let rest for 5 minutes, then place on a wire rack until completely cold. The cake will be very hot when it first comes out of the microwave, so be careful when handling it.

Heat the cream up until boiling. Place the chopped chocolate in a heatproof bowl and pour the hot cream over it. Let rest for 2 minutes, then stir very well until smooth.

Serve the chocolate sauce with the cake and scatter with rose petals, if you like.

In the past, when people asked me how to make ice cream without an ice-cream maker, I used to reply point-blank that, "No, no you can't, it won't work." Well, I am eating my words now. Not only does this recipe work, but it's wonderfully smooth and luscious. By serving it in cupcake papers, you can create a selection of different flavors from the same batch, so everyone can get their favorite. Here I'm making stracciatella (my favorite ice cream of all time), hokey pokey (vanilla with chocolate honeycomb pieces), and strawberry-marshmallow flavors.

NO-CHURN ICE CREAM "CUPCAKES"

MAKES 16

1 vanilla bean, split lengthways and seeds scraped out
1 tablespoon sugar
2½ cups (600 ml) heavy cream
1¼ cups (400 g) condensed milk
1¾ oz (50 g) dark chocolate, melted
4 strawberries, chopped
2 oz (60 g) mini marshmallows, or chopped regular marshmallows
1 chocolate honeycomb bar, such as Crunchie (or your favorite chocolate bar), chopped

Put the vanilla seeds and sugar in a small bowl and rub them through with your fingertips. This helps to separate the seeds, so they evenly flavor the ice cream.

In a stand mixer, or with electric beaters, whip your heavy cream with the vanilla sugar to soft peaks. Fold the cream into the condensed milk.

Place 16 cupcake papers in a cupcake or muffin pan and put a spoon of whipped cream and condensed milk in 4 of them. From a height, drizzle your melted chocolate over them, then add a second spoon of cream and drizzle with more chocolate: the thinner the layers and the more you add, the nicer this stracciatella will be.

Divide the rest of the ice cream mixture evenly between 2 bowls. Fold the strawberries and marshmallows into the first, then the chopped chocolate bar into the second. Spoon each of those mixtures evenly between 4 cupcake papers.

Place in the freezer for 2–3 hours, then serve.

About the author

Anna Haugh was born in Dublin in the 1980s. She has trained and worked as a professional chef for twenty years. After studying at DIT School of Culinary Arts and Food Technology—commonly known as Cathal Brugha Street—in Dublin, Anna began her career working at L'Ecrivain restaurant in Dublin with Derry Clarke. She then moved to London, where she worked with Shane Osborn at Pied à Terre, Philip Howard at The Square and for the Gordon Ramsay Group.

In May 2019, she opened Myrtle Restaurant in Chelsea, London. The name was inspired by the Irish chef Myrtle Allen, founder of Ballymaloe House. Anna takes inspiration from old Irish recipes, culture and stories to create a modern Irish cuisine that still has the heartbeat of home. At Myrtle Restaurant there is a large focus on great Irish produce, music and art.

Anna has worked on numerous television shows for the BBC. She is the resident chef on the breakfast show *Morning Live*, often appears as a chef and host on *Saturday Kitchen* and was a new *Masterchef: The Professionals* judge for 2022.

This is her first book.

Index

Acknowledgments

Go raibh mile maith agat.

In Ireland we say "thank you" in a wonderful way: it means "may there be a thousand goodnesses by you."

The people who helped me make this book should be thanked first. Lucy, who had to help navigate my words—from my mouth and on paper—into something coherent and well written. It's Lucy's talent for the inner story that you're reading.

Laura, my wonderful photographer that took my food and made it beautiful and added new levels to the feel of each dish.

Rosie, ably assisted by El, Lucy and Maria, who worked on the recipes with me and helped me question what a recipe should look like. Tabs, who has the eye for beauty and balance, with the addition of color or a textured napkin: her kindness radiates off her. Emily and Rowan from Bloombury, who believed I could create a great cookbook and helped me build a team to do that. Sabhbh, my literary agent, who helped me shape up the proposal to get publishers to turn the dream into a reality. Sandra, who took all of the above and wove each idea and concept together to create a flow that jumps off the page. This band of incredibly talented women worked with me to create this book. Now, being able to cook delicious food is one thing, but shaping that into a book that a home cook can follow is another. And not only follow, but fill with recipes that will inspire you to embark on something new. I couldn't have done this without them, I mean that from the bottom of my heart.

And now I must thank the people in my life. My mother, my first head chef, who taught me how to make stocks and jams, roast potatoes and cook real food from scratch. My father, who really taught me to have a curiosity about food, flavor and ingredients from all over the world. They were my first guinea pigs as I started to experiment in the kitchen. My sisters Catherine and Sarah, such keen home cooks, who through my entire career have motivated me to cook real tasty food, not just cheffy stuff. They challenge me and impress me beyond belief, both through the questions they ask me about cooking and the food they serve me: always—and I mean always—delicious. My brother Anthony, who when his beautiful wife Michelle passed away asked me the most basic cooking questions, as he now was in the kitchen cooking for his wonderful children Joe, Katelyn and Laila. It was in these conversations with Anthony that I learned which tips and tricks people needed to be told, in order to cook better at home.

My two best pals: Janice and Orla. These two are my cheerleaders. When I first moved to London, I was lonely. It was tough and I honestly could write a book just on that experience alone. I would go to a red phone box with a phone card on Sundays to call them; they would have been out partying the night before and we would all chat and laugh and I would often cry, out of pure gratitude for their friendship. They would tell me I was amazing and so brave and talented, even before I could properly chop an onion. You see, when the right people see your potential, you are unstoppable... but it was a long journey. Without them I'm not sure I'd have stuck it out.

Rich—now an honorary cheerleader, too—has been my dinner date for a decade, often joined by my stepson Henry, and we have a new recruit to eat my food in the form of a beautiful bubbly blonde boy called Oisín. Rich is navigating this busy life with me, and, without him, I'm not sure I could do it. If he didn't have my back, I wouldn't have achieved what I have. He is a brilliant dad and does more than most dads, I think. And that needs to be shouted from the rooftops.

I always say I was raised by three families: Mine, Janice's (my Uncle Tony and Aunty Marian), and Orla's parents Joe and Liz Dunne. Meal times in their house were all very different to mine, except for one core message. Their intention was just the same as that of my mammy and daddy: love, nourishment and sharing.

I want to thank those great chefs whose kitchens taught me resourcefulness and how not to waste: even in peeling there is the opportunity for creativity! So thank you Shane Osborn, Derry Clarke, Philip Howard, Rob Weston, Gordon Ramsay, Gualtiero Marchesi and Caroline Hall.

And finally, I'm so proud of my team at Myrtle: G-Bob, Ryanoooooo, Jimmy-Jam, Kennylicious, Jazzy Jeff and our manager, Dan. To see their excitement at this book coming together is something I didn't expect. Getting this book done involved a massive group effort from my kitchen. As I was prepping for the photo shoots, they were right behind me and never ever gave anything but encouragement. Thanks to Dan for always being a critical eye and a great ear to chew: you love food and recipes as much as I do. And Ash: thanks for all the coffee.